Crafts & More
for Children's Ministry

By Karyn Henley and Lois Keffer

Group®

Loveland, Colorado

Crafts & More for Children's Ministry
Copyright © 1993 Karyn Henley

First Printing

Credits
Edited by Jennifer Root Wilger
Interior designed by Dori Walker
Cover designed by Liz Howe
Cover photography by Jafe Parsons

Except where otherwise noted, scriptures are quoted from The Youth Bible, New Century Version, copyright © 1991 by Word Publishing, Dallas, Texas 75039. Used by permission.

Henley, Karyn.
      Crafts & more for children's ministry / by Karyn Henley and Lois Keffer.
         p.   cm.
      ISBN 1-55945-191-2
      1. Bible crafts. 2. Christian education of children. I. Title. II. Title Crafts & more for children's ministry.
      BS613.H46   1993
      268'.432—dc20   93-10755
                                                                              CIP

Printed in the United States of America

Contents

Introduction 5

OLD TESTAMENT

Cornstarch Swamp 9
   Creation

Traffic Sign Mobile 10
   Adam and Eve leave the garden

Pipe Cleaner Umbrella 12
   Noah

Paper-Cup Tower 13
   Tower of Babel

Follow the Trail.......................................14
   Abraham travels

Campfire Snack 15
   Abraham and the three visitors

Bottle-Cap Necklace 16
   A wife for Isaac

Up and Down...17
   Jacob deceives Isaac

Cloth Angel Puppets..................................18
   Jacob's dream

Star Patterns 19
   Joseph's dreams

Savings Bank 21
   Joseph's brothers

Helping Baskets.......................................22
   Baby Moses

Tissue Flames...24
   The burning bush

Button-Eyed Frogs.....................................25
   Plagues in Egypt

Cloud by Day, Fire by Night 26
   Crossing the Red Sea

Honey Cakes 27
   God sends manna

Toast Tablets 28
   The Ten Commandments

Communion Cup Print 29
   Twelve spies go into Canaan

Paper-Cup Donkeys 30
   Balaam's talking donkey

Hide the Spies 31
   Spies go into Jericho

Balloon Sunshine 32
   The sun stands still

Against the Odds......................................33
   Gideon

Samson Hair 34
   Samson

Grain Painting...36
   Ruth gathers grain

Big Ears 37
   Samuel hears God

Can You See Through This? 38
   David is anointed king

Shield of Faith 39
   David and Goliath

Braided Belt..40
   David and Jonathan

Abigail Snack 41
   David and Abigail

English Muffin Owls 42
   Solomon chooses wisdom

Origami Birds...43
   Elijah is fed by birds

Reinforcer Altar 45
   Elijah and the prophets of Baal

Paper-Cup Chariot....................................46
   Elijah goes into heaven

Model House 46
   Elisha is given a room on a roof

Dyeing Eggs 48
   Naaman

Scroll Rolls 49
   Josiah

Self-Control Trail Mix 50
   Daniel refuses the king's food

Shield Tag 51
   The fiery furnace

Corncake Lions 52
   Daniel in the lions' den

Building and Measuring............................53
   Rebuilding the walls of Jerusalem

Cheese Fries..54
   Jonah

NEW TESTAMENT

Popcorn Name 59
  The birth of John the Baptist

Who Brought the Message? 60
  Gabriel announces Jesus' birth to Mary

Manger Cards 61
  Jesus' birth

Graham Cracker Stable 62
  Shepherds visit baby Jesus

Wise Men Cups 64
  Wise men visit baby Jesus

The Carpenter's Shop 65
  Jesus grows up

Starting Off Right 66
  Jesus is baptized

Caterpillar to Butterfly 67
  Jesus changes water into wine

Tin Can Lanterns 68
  Nicodemus visits Jesus

Mirror Image 69
  Jesus calls Peter, Andrew, James, and John

Around Together 70
  Jesus chooses apostles

Flower Cookies 71
  Jesus teaches about the lilies of the field

Do You Believe? 72
  The centurion's servant

Seeds 73
  The sower and the seed

Storm in a Jar 74
  Jesus stills the storm

Vanilla-Wafer Sandwiches 75
  Jesus feeds the 5,000

Walking Across 76
  Jesus walks on water

Hands Wreath 78
  The good Samaritan

I Can Help 79
  Mary and Martha

Popcorn Cones 81
  A rich man builds bigger barns

Find a Coin 82
  The lost coin

Heart Stencil 83
  The lost son

Thank You Envelopes 84
  The 10 sick men

Prayer Booklet 86
  The Pharisee and the tax collector pray

Getting to the Treasure 87
  Jesus and the children

Blind Tag 88
  Jesus heals a blind man

Cone Trees 89
  Zacchaeus

Bread-Stick Faces 90
  Jesus raises Lazarus

Clothespin Donkey 91
  Jesus enters Jerusalem on a colt

Cinnamon Cookies 92
  The widow's offering

Soap and Water 93
  Jesus washes the disciples' feet

Reminders 94
  The Last Supper

Tree of Life 95
  The Crucifixion

Paper Angels 96
  The angel at the tomb

Joy Biscuits 97
  Peter and John heal a man who couldn't walk

Chariot Wheels 98
  Philip and the Ethiopian

Silhouettes 99
  Paul on the road to Damascus

Ball Toss 101
  Paul escapes in a basket

Bandannas 102
  Dorcas is raised from death

Prayer Partners 103
  Peter escapes from prison

Dyed Wind-Flags 105
  Lydia becomes a Christian

Missionary Map 106
  Paul's missionary journeys

Go to Jail 108
  Paul and Silas in jail

Riding a Storm 109
  Paul's shipwreck

Fruit of the Spirit Mural 110
  The fruit of the Spirit

Introduction

How many times have you looked through piles of books to find a craft or an activity to reinforce a Bible story?

Well, look no further. In this book you'll find 86 new Bible crafts and activities. Each activity is paired with a Bible story and discussion questions to help kids remember and apply the story's truth to their lives.

You'll enjoy using *Crafts & More for Children's Ministry* with children in elementary school. These activities will add life to your Bible stories in Sunday school, vacation Bible school, midweek club, or any time kids come together. The activities call for easy-to-find materials you can gather quickly. Bible references are provided for you to read the stories straight from the Bible. Or, if you'd prefer, read the stories from a Bible storybook or tell them in your own words.

You'll find something for every student in *Crafts & More for Children's Ministry*. A variety of games, crafts, cooking, and science activities will appeal to all five senses. And the more senses kids use, the more they learn.

So dig right in! You'll enjoy watching your kids grow as they hear, see, touch, smell, and taste the truths of God's Word!

Old Testament

Cornstarch Swamp

STORY

Creation (Genesis 1:1–2:3)

At God's command, stars glowed, mountains rose, rivers flowed, plants grew, and animals roamed. As children compare their creative efforts to God's creative power, they'll be inspired to marvel at God's greatness.

THE EXPERIENCE

Tell the story of Creation found in Genesis 1:1–2:3.

Ask:

● **If you closed your eyes and imagined a movie about Creation, what would you see?** (Volcanoes; lightning; plants growing.)

● **How can God create something from nothing?** (I don't know; because he's God; God has great power.)

● **Can people create something from nothing?** (No, we have to have ingredients; we can use things God made.)

Say: **Let's see what we can create today with the ingredients I've brought.**

Spread newspapers over the table. Give children each a cup, a spoon, and a plate. In each cup, put ¼ cup cornstarch and ⅛ cup water. Help children stir the mixture well and pour it onto the plate.

Ask:

● **What is a swamp?** (Swamps are muddy; swamps have alligators; swamps have lots of water and grass.)

● **Have you ever seen a swamp? Where?** (On TV; at the zoo; in my back yard when it rained all day.)

● **How is this mixture like a swamp?** (It's mushy; it feels slimy; it's like mud.)

Encourage children to explore the swamp mixture by touching it with their fingers, trying to roll it into a ball, or holding it in their hands.

Ask:

● **What's the difference between the way God creates and the way we create?** (We have to have something to make something, but God made something from nothing.)

Say: **Today we learned how powerful God is. God created everything. Let's say a prayer of thanks for all the great things God created.**

Let children take their mixtures home or dispose of them and recycle the plates.

Traffic Sign Mobile

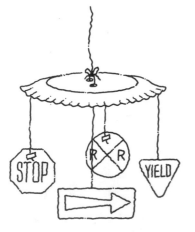

STORY

Adam and Eve leave the garden (Genesis 2:15-17; 3:1-24)

When Adam and Eve disobeyed God and ate fruit from the tree of the knowledge of good and evil, God sent them out of the beautiful garden that had been their home. Children will see that God takes disobedience seriously and learn the importance of obeying God.

THE EXPERIENCE

Tell the story of Adam and Eve leaving the garden, found in Genesis 2:15-17; 3:1-24.

Ask:

● **Why do you think God said not to eat fruit from that one tree?** (God knew they'd be happier if they didn't eat from it; God wanted to see if they would obey.)

● **Do you think the serpent made Eve disobey? Why?** (Yes, he tempted her; no, Eve decided to disobey; Eve could have said no.)

● **What are some rules we have to follow?** (Classroom rules; rules at home; traffic rules.)

Say: **We're going to make a mobile that will remind us about obeying rules.**

Give children each a photocopy of the "Traffic Signs" handout and a half sheet of red, yellow, and white construction paper. Help children identify the "stop," "yield," "one way," and "railroad crossing" sign shapes. Have children cut out the shapes from their handouts and trace them on the correct color of construction paper. Distribute crayons or markers and help children label their traffic sign shapes. Be sure to help younger children who haven't learned to write yet.

Give children each a plate and four 18-inch lengths of string. Show them how to tape one end of each string to the plate, and the other end to a sign. Give children each an additional string and help them loop it through the holes in the plate and tie the loose ends together.

Ask:

● **Tell us about some traffic rules you know.** (Cars have to stop at stop signs and red lights; look both ways before you cross the street.)

● **What would happen if cars and bicycles had no rules to follow?** (Nobody would know what to do; people would crash.)

● **Why do people make traffic rules?**

● **Why does God make rules for us?** (Because God loves us; because God doesn't want us to be hurt.)

Form pairs. Say: **Tell your partner one way you can obey God's rules this week.**

Close in prayer, thanking God for giving us rules to help and protect us.

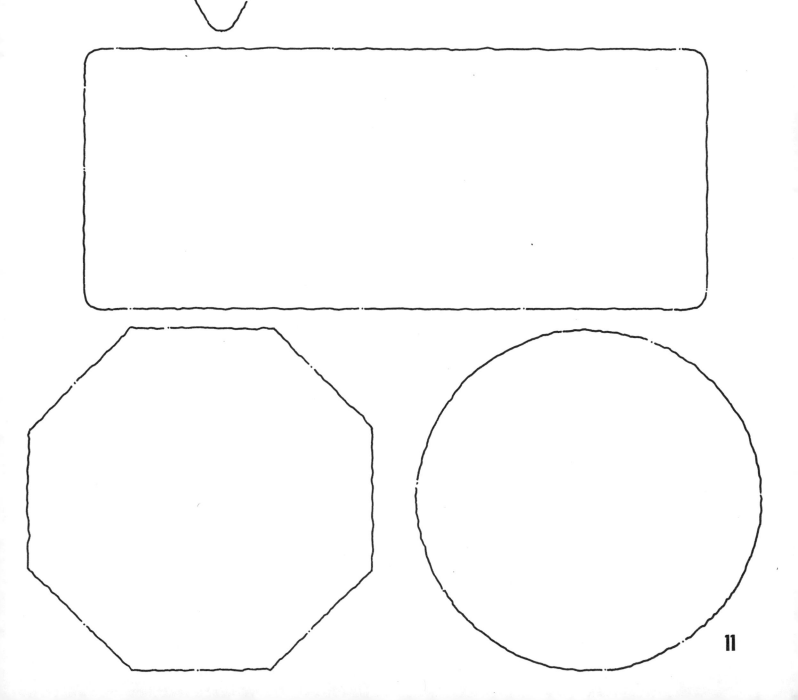

Traffic Signs

Pipe Cleaner Umbrella

PREPARATION

You'll need:

- pipe cleaners,
- large paper baking cups,
- and crayons or markers.

STORY

Noah (Genesis 6:5–8:22)

When God told Noah to build a huge boat, Noah obeyed. God then sent a flood to destroy all living things on earth. But he saved Noah and all who were aboard the boat. Knowing that God took care of Noah helps children understand that God takes care of us, too.

THE EXPERIENCE

Ask:

- **When might people be afraid?** (In the dark; in scary movies; in thunder and lightning.)
- **What kinds of storms have you been in?** (Tornadoes; thunderstorms; hurricanes; blizzards.)
- **What are some things that protect us in storms?** (Our houses; raincoats; umbrellas.)

Say: **We're going to make umbrellas to remind us of God's protection, then we'll hear a story about a man God protected from a storm.**

Give each child a baking cup, a pipe cleaner, and crayons or markers. Have children each color their own designs on the outside of the baking cup, turn it upside down, and slide a pipe cleaner through the center. Show them how to make a small loop in the pipe cleaner above the cup, and a curve in the pipe cleaner at the other end.

Tell the story of Noah, found in Genesis 6:5–8:22. Have children hold up their umbrellas each time you say "rain" or "flood." If you have another teacher or helper in your class, have that person flash the lights to create "lightning" for the storm.

Ask:

- **What could Noah have been afraid of?** (Wind; rain; thunder; the wild animals.)
- **How did God take care of Noah?** (God told him to build the ark; God kept the ark from sinking.)
- **When we're afraid, what can we do?** (Pray; call a friend or parent.)

Form pairs. Have kids tell their partners about a time they were afraid and someone took care of them.

Say: **Every time it rains, think about your umbrella and God's promise of protection. God takes care of us when we're afraid.**

Paper-Cup Tower

STORY

The tower of Babel (Genesis 11:1-9)

People began building a tall tower to "make a name for themselves." But when God saw their selfishness and pride, he confused their languages, and they stopped building. Use this story to teach children that God wants them to be humble, not proud.

THE EXPERIENCE

Tell the story of the tower of Babel, found in Genesis 11:1-9.
Ask:

● **How do you think God felt about the people's plans to build a tower? Explain.** (God was angry; God didn't let them finish their tower.)

● **Why do you think God stopped the people from finishing the tower?** (God wanted to show them that he's the one in charge; the tower was getting too tall.)

Say: **We're going to build our own towers today. I've invited a building supervisor to help us.** Introduce the person who speaks another language, but don't tell the children that this person speaks another language.

Form two groups and give each group 50 cups. Say: **When I say, "go," start building your towers. Make a row of cups, then stack another row on top of the first row. Stack as many rows as you can, and try to finish before the other group.**

Say "go" as soon as the groups are ready. Have the supervisor watch the building process until the children have two or three stories of cups stacked up. Then have the supervisor begin shaking his or her head and giving the children instructions in a different language. If you don't have a supervisor, instruct the children with nonsense words, such as "Tersel volet yawa. Noomek ingmov semak."

When the first tower is completed, or when the children have been trying for awhile, stop the building and ask:

● **How did you feel when you couldn't understand what the building supervisor was telling you?** (Confused; frustrated; it was funny; I didn't know what to do.)

● **How is that like the people who built the tower in the story might have felt?** (They probably felt the same way; they might have felt worse because they couldn't even talk to each other.)

● **Do you think the people could have ever made themselves as big or as important as God? Why or why not?** (No, because there's only one God; I'm not sure.)

● **Have you ever known people who try to be better than everyone else? Is it fun to be around people like that? Explain.**

13

(No, because they always brag; sometimes they do dangerous things to prove they're great.)

Read Matthew 20:26. If you have older children in your class, ask a volunteer to read it.

Say: **The people in our story thought building a big building would make them great. Let's remember what kind of people Jesus thinks are great and try to serve others this week.**

Follow the Trail

- -

PREPARATION

You'll need:

● masking tape

● and a bag of Hershey's Kisses or other individually wrapped candy.

● Before class, remove 10 to 15 Kisses from the bag. Use these Kisses to mark a trail. If you place the Kisses far apart, put masking tape arrows on the floor between them. At the end of the trail, hide the bag of Kisses. This activity will be more fun if you can hide the bag of Kisses in another room in the church building.

STORY

Abraham travels (Genesis 12:1-9)

Abraham waited for God's direction as he moved from place to place. Although the children in your class probably won't hear directions from God, they can read God's directions in the Bible. Use this story to encourage children to follow God's directions.

THE EXPERIENCE

Ask:

● **Has your family ever moved before? Where did you move?** (We moved to a new house; we moved to a different city.)

● **When you moved, did you know where you were going? Explain.** (I didn't know exactly where we were going, but I had an idea; I knew the name of my new street.)

● **What would you want to take with you if you moved?** (Toys; my bed; my family; my bike.)

● **When people move today, what do they pack their things in?** (A suitcase; a big truck; a duffel bag.)

● **How do you think people packed during Bible times?** (They carried things on camels and donkeys; they wrapped stuff up in their tents.)

Say: **Pack up any belongings you've brought with you. We're going on a journey.**

Have children line up. Lead them to the first marker, then let one of the children lead the group to the next marker. Continue until you've reached the last marker and found the bag of Hershey's Kisses. Distribute the Kisses, then have children sit on the floor in the new location.

● **What was it like to go on a journey and not know what you'd find at the end?** (Fun; exciting; scary.)

Say: **Our story today is about a man who followed God's directions and moved to a new place.**

Tell the story of Abraham's move, found in Genesis 12:1-9. After the story, ask:

● **How did Abraham know where to go?** (God showed him the way; he knew God had someplace in mind.)

● **God gave Abraham directions. Does God give us directions? How?** (Yes, God gives us directions in the Bible; God gives us directions by answering our prayers; no, God doesn't talk to us like he talked to Abraham.)

Say: **God gave Abraham directions about where to go, and when. Abraham followed God, God blessed Abraham. We can read the Bible, God's Word, and find out God's directions for living. If we follow the directions in the Bible, God will bless us.**

Campfire Snack

STORY

Abraham and the three visitors (Genesis 18:1-15)

Abraham invited three travelers to stop at his tent to rest and eat. Children may not be able to open their homes as Abraham did, but they can share their rooms, toys, and after-school snacks with friends. Use Abraham's example to encourage children to show kindness to visitors wherever they may find them. If you have visitors in your class today, encourage children to practice what they learn by helping the visitors feel at home.

THE EXPERIENCE

Ask:

● **What's it like to visit someone else's house?** (Fun to see someone else's room and toys; kind of hard to follow the rules at someone else's house.)

● **What do you do when you have a friend over?** (Play; eat lunch; watch videos.)

Say: **Sometimes people share a meal together to make visitors feel welcome in their house. We call that hospitality. Let's make a snack to share together while we listen to a story about someone who showed hospitality.**

Have children wash their hands, then set out the four large bowls. Let kids fill one large bowl with Chex cereal, one with pretzels, one with peanuts, and one with sunflower seeds. Then distribute cups and demonstrate how to put in a little of each ingredient.

Have children sit in a circle on the floor while they eat their snacks. Build a "campfire" by stacking the building blocks around the flashlights, then turn on the flashlights and tell the story of Abraham and his three visitors, found in Genesis 18:1-15.

Ask:

● **Do you think Abraham was expecting guests? Why or why**

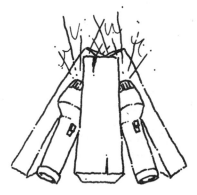

not? (No, he was just sitting around when they came; yes, he ran to meet them right away.)

● **Why do you think Abraham asked them to stay?** (He wanted company; he knew they must be tired and hungry.)

● **Can you think of a time someone made you feel welcome? Tell about it.**

● **What are some places besides home that we can make people feel welcome?** (We can welcome new kids at school; we can share our lunch with someone who forgot; we can welcome kids to our class at church.)

● **What can we do to make visitors feel welcome in our class?** (Help them meet friends; show them where everything is; get a chair for them; smile.)

Say: **Abraham made his visitors feel welcome. He showed hospitality. Let's practice hospitality by helping new friends feel welcome in our class.**

Bottle-Cap Necklace

PREPARATION

You'll need:

● **a 28-inch length of string**

● **and a protective ring-collar from the cap of a milk jug for each child.**

You'll also need:

● **newspaper,**

● **two small margarine cups,**

● **glitter,**

● **glue,**

● **and paper lunch bags.**

● **Spread the newspaper on the table where you'll be working.**

● **Pour the glue into the margarine cups and pour the glitter into the lunch bags.**

STORY

A wife for Isaac (Genesis 24)

Abraham sent his servant to find a wife for Isaac. The servant prayed for God's help, and God heard and answered his prayer. Children can learn from the servant's story to pray and look for God's answers.

THE EXPERIENCE

Tell the story of the servant's search, found in Genesis 24. You may need to condense this story, but be sure to include all references to the servant's gifts.

Ask:

● **Why did the servant pray?** (He wanted God to help him find a wife for Isaac; he wanted to make a wise decision.)

● **How do you think the servant felt when God answered his prayer?** (Good; thankful; surprised.)

Say: **We're going to make some necklaces to remind us of the jewelry Abraham's servant gave Rebekah and her family.**

Give children each a ring-collar and a string. Demonstrate how to run the string through the ring and tie the ends together. Dip the ring into the glue, then into the bag of glitter. Demonstrate how to close the top of the bag around the string and gently shake the bag. Lay the necklaces on the newspaper to dry.

Ask:

● **When can we pray? Where? How?** (We can pray any time; we can pray wherever we are; we can just talk to God like any other friend.)

● **Why does God want us to pray?** (So we'll talk to God; so we'll remember God's in charge.)

● **What kinds of prayers are there besides prayers asking God to do something for us?** (Asking God to help other people; thankful prayers; praising God.)

Form pairs and have kids tell a partner about a time God answered one of their prayers.

Say: **Let your jewelry be a reminder of how God hears and answers prayers. When you pray this week, look for the answers God gives.**

protective ring

necklace

Up and Down

STORY

Jacob deceives Isaac (Genesis 27:1-45)

Jacob, disguised as his brother Esau, went to Isaac to receive the family blessing. Isaac, old and blind, gave Jacob the blessing. Children will see how many people can be hurt by a lie and learn the importance of telling the truth.

THE EXPERIENCE

Say: **Before our story, we're going to play a guessing game. First, we need to learn a simple Bible verse. It's found in Ephesians 4:25 (NIV), and it's only two words long. The verse says, "Speak truthfully."**

Have the children repeat the verse with you several times. Then direct them to sit in a circle on the floor. Choose one child to be "It." Have It sit or stand in the middle of the circle, eyes closed.

Say: **I'm going to tap someone's shoulder. If I tap you, you must say the Bible verse. You can either stand up or sit down to say it. The person in the middle will try to guess who is speaking and whether the speaker is sitting or standing. If you want, you can try to disguise your voice so It won't recognize you. If It guesses correctly, he or she gets to trade places with the person who said the verse. If It makes a wrong guess, he or she is It again. A person can only be It two times in a row.**

Play the game until everyone has had a chance to be It.

Ask:

● **What's the difference between fooling someone and lying?** (They're the same, fooling someone is lying; fooling *is* usually just for fun.)

● **Did you ever find out someone lied to you? How did you feel?** (Angry; sad that the person was afraid to tell me the truth.)

Say: **Lying makes everyone feel bad. Our story today is about a**

man who told a lie to his father.

Tell the story of how Jacob deceived Isaac, found in Genesis 27:1-45. Ask:

● **How do you think Isaac felt when he found out Jacob had lied?** (Disappointed that his son wanted to trick him; sad that he couldn't give another blessing to Esau.)

● **How did Esau feel when he found out Jacob had lied?** (Mad at himself for letting Jacob trick him; mad at Jacob for stealing something that was his.)

● **What happened to Jacob because of his lie?** (His brother wanted to kill him; he had to run away; he lost contact with his family.)

● **Why did Jacob lie?** (Because he was greedy; he wanted something that belonged to his brother.)

● **Is it always easy to tell the truth? Why or why not?** (No, sometimes you think a lie will keep you out of trouble; sometimes the truth is embarrassing; yes, I know I'll get in trouble if I lie.)

Say: **Many people were hurt because Jacob lied. Let's remember to speak truthfully.**

Cloth Angel Puppets

PREPARATION

For each child, you'll need:

● a handkerchief or an 8×8-inch square of white fabric,

● a large cotton ball,

● string or ribbon,

● scissors,

● and a 4×6 unlined index card with two holes punched in the center.

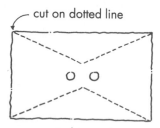

cut on dotted line

index card

STORY

Jacob's dream (Genesis 28:10-22)

Jacob was traveling. When he lay down to sleep, he dreamed of angels on a stairway going into heaven. God promised to be with Jacob wherever he went. Hearing about God's care for Jacob assures children God will be with them wherever they are, too.

THE EXPERIENCE

Ask:

● **Where do you like to travel?** (To visit my cousins; to the beach; to the mountains; to Disneyland.)

● **How does it feel to sleep in a different bed with a different pillow?** (Strange; uncomfortable; fun.)

Say: **Today we're going to hear a story about a traveling man who slept one night on a very different kind of pillow. But first, we're going to make some puppets to help us tell the story.**

Give each child a square of cloth, a cotton ball, an 8-inch length of string, a pair of scissors and an index card. Show children how to cut a V-shape at the top and bottom of the index card to make angel wings.

Have children thread the string or ribbon through the holes in the wings, leaving a loop in front. Then help them place their cotton balls in the center of their cloth squares, gather the cloth up around the cotton ball, slip the cotton ball into the loop of string, and tie the string behind the wings. Be sure children tie the string loosely so they'll be able to put a finger into the cotton ball.

Tell the story of Jacob's dream, found in Genesis 28:10-22. Have the children fly their angels up and down when you tell about Jacob's dream.

Ask:

● **How would you feel if you had a dream like Jacob's?** (Scared; like I was in heaven; excited; confused.)

● **Can you tell about a time God took care of you when you were traveling?** (Once our car went off the road, but nobody got hurt; once we ran out of gas, but we were right by a gas station.)

● **Do you think God can take care of you anywhere?** (Yes, God knows where we are all the time; God is everywhere; no, God might not have time to go everywhere with everyone.)

Say: **Let your angels remind you that God watches over you wherever you go, just as he watched over Jacob.**

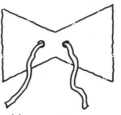

ribbon or string runs
through holes

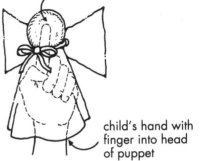

cotton ball inside

child's hand with
finger into head
of puppet

Star Patterns

- -

STORY

Joseph's dreams (Genesis 37:1-11)

When Joseph told his family about his dreams they became jealous of him rather than rejoicing with him. Use this story to encourage children to be happy instead of jealous when good things happen to their friends.

THE EXPERIENCE

Ask:

● **Have you ever looked through a telescope at the sky? If so, what did you see?** (Lots of stars; the Milky Way; the moon looked really big.)

Say: **The patterns stars make in the sky are called constellations. After we make booklets of these star patterns, we'll hear about someone in the Bible who had a dream about the stars.**

Have children fold two sheets of black construction paper in half to make a booklet. Punch two holes along each booklet's fold. Have children thread a 12-inch length of yarn through the holes and tie a bow on the outside of their booklets.

Give children each a photocopy of the "Star Patterns" handout. If you've brought science books or encyclopedias, show pictures of constellations from the books. Have children copy constellations from the "Star Patterns" handout by placing star stickers in the right spots in their booklets. Help children write the names of constellations they've copied with a yellow or white crayon. As children work, emphasize the fact that God created these beautiful star patterns.

PREPARATION

You'll need:

● black construction paper,

● photocopies of the "Star Patterns" handout (p. 20),

● a hole punch,

● yarn,

● scissors,

● star stickers,

● and yellow or white crayons.

You may also want to bring:

● books that show maps of star constellations, such as encyclopedias or science books.

STAR PATTERNS

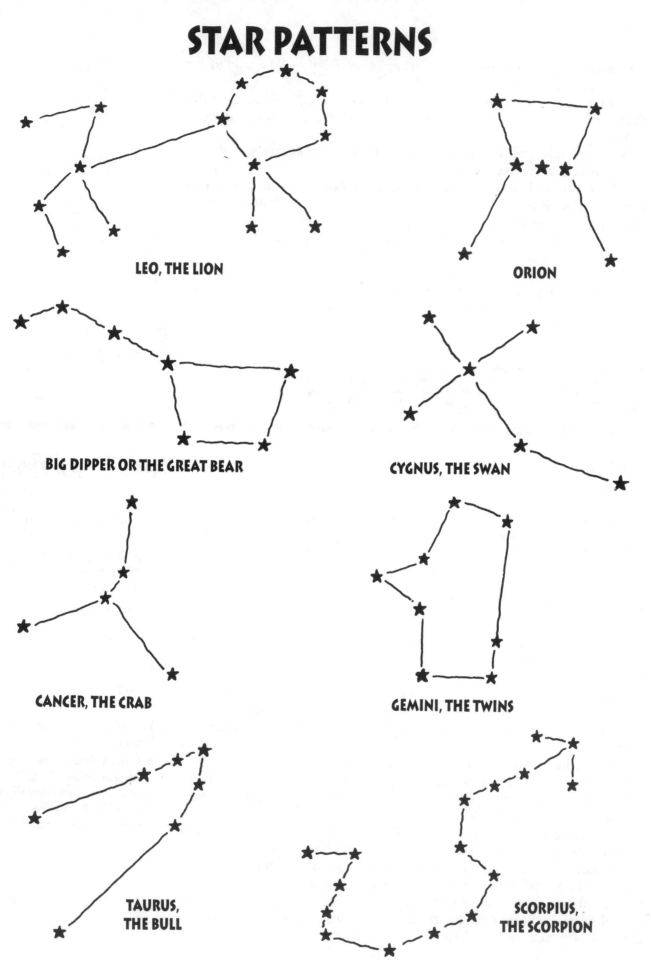

LEO, THE LION

ORION

BIG DIPPER OR THE GREAT BEAR

CYGNUS, THE SWAN

CANCER, THE CRAB

GEMINI, THE TWINS

TAURUS,
THE BULL

SCORPIUS,
THE SCORPION

Tell the story of Joseph's dreams, found in Genesis 37:1-11.

Ask:

● **Why do you think Joseph told his dreams to his family?** (To brag; to see what they thought.)

● **How do you think he felt when his brothers hated him because of his dreams?** (Sorry he said anything; sad; frustrated.)

● **Is it easy or hard to be happy when a friend has good news and you don't? Why?** (Hard, because I wish the good news had happened to me; easy, because I want my friends to be happy, too.)

Say: **We're often tempted to be jealous when someone else tells us about a good thing that has happened. But how would that make them feel?** (Sad; sorry they said something.)

Read Romans 12:15. If you have older students in your class, ask a volunteer to read it.

Say: **When you see the stars in your booklet or in the sky, remember Joseph's story and be happy for other people's good news.**

Savings Bank

STORY

Joseph's brothers (Genesis 42–45 and 50:15-21)

Joseph's brothers hated him and sold him into slavery. Years later, they had to depend on Joseph to provide them with food for their families. When children hear how Joseph forgave his brothers, they'll realize that they, too, can forgive others, even when it seems hard.

THE EXPERIENCE

Ask:

● **Tell about a time you saved money for something. What did you save for?** (A new bike; Nintendo; money to spend on vacation.)

Say: **We're going to make savings banks. Then we'll hear a story about how some people in the Bible used the money they saved.**

Distribute margarine tubs and help children cut slits in the lids. Show children how to cut a variety of small shapes out of Con-Tac paper, peel off the backing, and stick the shapes around the sides and on top of the margarine tubs.

As children are finishing their banks, tell the story of Joseph found in Genesis 42–45 and 50:15-21. Emphasize how Joseph put his brothers' money back in their sacks, then later revealed himself to them and forgave them.

Ask:

● **What would have happened if Joseph hadn't forgiven his brothers?** (His brothers wouldn't have any food; his brothers would

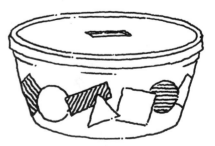

have been in trouble.)

● **When you don't forgive, what happens in your own heart?** (You get angry and bitter; you're not happy.)

● **Is it always easy for you to forgive? Why or why not?** (No, sometimes I'm too mad at the person; I usually do it because I know I should, but it's hard.)

● **Why is it important to forgive others?** (So we can be peaceful and happy; because God forgives us.)

Say: **Joseph had a good reason to be angry at his brothers, but he forgave them. God blessed Joseph and his brothers for making peace by forgiving. Each time you put a coin in your bank, think of someone you need to forgive. Ask God to help you forgive that person.**

Helping Baskets

PREPARATION

You'll need:

● **a margarine tub**

● **and a photocopy of the "Helping Baskets" handout (p. 23) for each child,**

● **various colors of large construction paper,**

● **scissors,**

● **and a stapler.**

● **Before class, cut the construction paper lengthwise into half-inch strips. Cut slits around the sides of each margarine tub.**

STORY

Baby Moses (Exodus 1:6–2:10)

Miriam helped her mother by watching baby Moses as he floated in a basket on the river. Because Miriam was nearby, she was able to bring her mother to the princess to take care of the baby. Children will learn from this story that good things happen when they help others.

THE EXPERIENCE

Ask:

● **What do you do to help at home?** (Clean up my room; help do the dishes; set the table.)

Say: **Our story today is about a girl who helped by watching her baby brother.**

Tell the story of baby Moses, found in Exodus 1:6–2:10.

Ask:

● **Why do you think Miriam agreed to look after her brother?** (To make sure he'd be safe; to help her mom; so she could play by the river.)

● **How do you think Miriam felt when she saw the princess pick up Moses?** (Scared; excited; curious.)

● **What good things happened because of Miriam's helpfulness?** (Her mother got to be with Moses again; she got to meet the princess; she made sure Moses didn't fall in the water.)

Say: **We're going to make baskets that will remind us to be helpful, like Miriam.**

Give children each a margarine tub and several construction paper strips. Show them how to weave the strips through the slits in the margarine tubs to make baskets. Cut several strips in half to use as

HELPING BASKETS

I'LL CLEAN MY ROOM.

I'LL SET THE TABLE.

I'LL HELP WITH THE DISHES.

I'LL GIVE YOU A BACK RUB.

handles and staple a handle to each child's basket.

Give each child a photocopy of the "Helping Baskets" handout. Say: **The strips on your handout tell different ways you can help your family. You can fill in more ways to help on the blank strips. Cut out the strips and put them in your basket. Show the basket to your family and have them draw a strip whenever they need help.**

As children are working, help them think of specific ways they can help their families. For example, if they have younger siblings, they could help by playing with a brother or sister while their parents are busy.

When children have finished cutting out their strips, say: **Remember the good things that happened when Miriam was helpful. When you help others, good things will happen in your family, too.**

Tissue Flames

PREPARATION

You'll need:

- **paper bowls,**
- **glue,**
- **water,**
- **paintbrushes,**
- **white construction paper,**
- **scissors,**
- **and red and yellow tissue paper.**
- **Using the "Flame Pattern" shown below as a guide, cut flame shapes out of the tissue paper.**

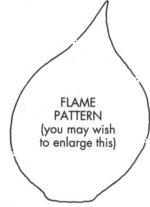

FLAME
PATTERN
(you may wish
to enlarge this)

STORY

The burning bush (Exodus 3–4)

Moses approached what he thought was just a burning bush, and he heard the voice of God. God requested that Moses remove his shoes, and out of respect for God's holiness, Moses obeyed. Children will learn from Moses' example to respect and worship God.

THE EXPERIENCE

Ask:

- **What is respect?** (Being kind; politeness; thoughtfulness; thinking someone's great.)
- **Who do you respect?** (My parents; my grandpa; my teachers at school.)
- **How can we show respect for others?** (Listen to them; be polite; do things for them.)

Say: **Our story today is about a man who showed respect for God.**

Tell the story of the burning bush, found in Exodus 3–4.

Say: **While we talk about this story, let's make a collage of flames to remind us of the burning bush.**

Give each child a sheet of white construction paper and a paintbrush. Set out bowls containing a mixture of one part glue and one part water. Then set out the tissue flames. Show children how to place yellow and red flames on the paper at random, then paint over the flames with the glue mixture. The overlap of the yellow and the red flames should produce orange flames.

As children work, ask:

- **Why do you think God asked Moses to take off his shoes?**

(To show respect; so his shoes wouldn't burn.)

● **Moses showed respect for God by taking off his shoes. How can we show respect for God today?** (Praise God; worship God; speak respectfully about God; bow our heads when we pray.)

Say: **When you see your tissue flames, remember Moses and the burning bush. Moses showed great respect for God. God is awesome, powerful, and loving. God deserves our respect, too.**

paint on with glue/water

Button-Eyed Frogs

STORY

Plagues in Egypt (Exodus 5–11; 12:29-32)

God sent plagues to Egypt to convince Pharaoh to let God's people go. After each plague, Pharaoh would agree, only to change his mind the next day. When children see how Moses was persistent in the face of discouragement, they'll be encouraged to be persistent, too.

THE EXPERIENCE

Ask:
● **Can you make a sound like a frog?**
● **What else do you know about frogs?**

Say: **We're going to make some button-eyed frogs, then we'll hear a story about frogs that were not welcome.**

Give children each a sheet of construction paper and a crayon. Show children how to draw a frog by drawing a large circle with a small circle above it and two triangles below it. Have children glue on buttons as eyes, draw mouths, and color their frogs.

Tell the story of the 10 plagues, found in Exodus 5–11; 12:29-32. Encourage children to hold up their frogs and say "ribbit" when you tell about the plague of frogs.

Ask:
● **What does it mean to be discouraged?** (To think about quitting or giving up; to think you won't be able to do something.)
● **What reasons did Moses have to be discouraged?** (Pharaoh kept changing his mind; it took so long to convince Pharaoh.)
● **Why didn't Moses give up?** (Because God promised to help him; because he knew God would keep on making plagues until Pharaoh let the people go.)

Say: **Moses didn't give up, even though he had a hard job to do. Because Moses kept trying, Pharaoh eventually let God's people go. Write on your frog one hard job you might have to do this week. When you're faced with that hard job, think of Moses, and don't give up!**

PREPARATION

You'll need:

● **light-colored construction paper,**
● **crayons,**
● **buttons,**
● **and glue.**

Cloud by Day, Fire by Night

PREPARATION

You'll need:

- white construction paper,
- drinking straws,
- scissors,
- red and yellow crayons,
- tape,
- glue,
- and cotton balls.

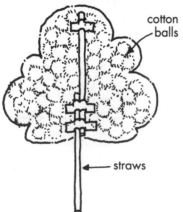

cotton balls

straws

STORY

Crossing the Red Sea (Exodus 13:21-22 and 14:1-31)

God guided his people in the wilderness by a cloud in the daytime and a pillar of fire at night. God also used the cloud to shield the Israelites from the Egyptian army. When children see how God guided the Israelites, they'll be encouraged to look to God for guidance in their own lives.

THE EXPERIENCE

Ask:

- **Did you ever take a night hike and use a flashlight to help guide you? What was it like?** (Dark; scary; there were lots of shadows.)

Say: **Flashlights are a great guide for walking at night. We're going to hear a story today about an unusual light that guided God's people in the desert.**

Tell the story of the cloud, the pillar of fire, and the crossing of the Red Sea found in Exodus 13:21-22 and 14:1-31.

Ask:

- **What do you think it would have been like to follow a cloud and to see a pillar of fire at night?** (Exciting; scary; awesome.)

Say: **We're going to make a paper cloud and pillar to remind us of this story, then we'll play a game to see what it was like to follow a cloud.**

Give children each a pair of scissors and sheet of white paper. Show them how to cut out a large cloud shape. Have children color one side of the cloud with red and yellow crayons to make it look like the pillar of fire.

Have children each tape one straw to the back of their cloud and glue cotton balls around it. Have them tape another straw to the bottom of the cloud to make a handle.

Say: **Now we're going to play a Follow the Leader game. The leader will hold up his or her cloud. When the leader's cloud stops, everyone stops. When the leader's cloud moves, everyone moves.**

Choose a leader and play the game. Then ask:

- **What is a guide?** (A leader; someone who knows more than you.)
- **When do we need a guide the most?** (When we don't know which way to go; when we want to know more; at a museum; on a hike.)
- **How does God guide us?** (God gives us parents and teachers; we

can learn what God wants us to do by reading the Bible.)

Say: **God has always been a guide for his people. When you see clouds this week, remember that just as God guided the Israelites, God will guide you.**

Honey Cakes

STORY

God sends manna (Exodus 16)

When God's people complained about missing the food they ate in Egypt, God wasn't happy. But because God loved them, God graciously sent them food. Hearing about the complaints of God's people will remind children to be content with what they have.

THE EXPERIENCE

Ask:
● **What is complaining?** (Whining; griping; saying something's not the way you like it.)
● **What do people usually complain about?** (Weather; other people; school; work.)

Say: **We're going to hear a story about a time God's people complained. But first let's make some honey cakes.**

Preheat the oven to 350 degrees.

Have children wash their hands. Help one group of children measure and mix the melted butter, honey, cinnamon, and vanilla in a bowl. Help another group measure and mix the baking mix and milk in another bowl, then have the first group add their butter-and-honey mixture. Help children mix the ingredients well.

Give children each a small portion of dough on a paper plate. Show them how to roll the dough into a ball, place it on the cookie sheet, and press it down lightly. Bake the honey cakes at 350 degrees for 10 minutes, then enjoy. If there's no oven in your room, ask a teacher or assistant to take the cakes to an oven and bring them back when they're done.

As the honey cakes are baking, tell the story of God's sending manna to his people, found in Exodus 16.

As kids are eating their honey cakes, ask:
● **Were God's people right to complain? Why or why not?** (No, because God helped them get out of Egypt; God was taking care of them all along; yes, the food they had in the desert was probably pretty bad.)
● **What's wrong with complaining?** (Complaining makes everyone feel bad; it might show you're not trusting God; you're not thankful when you complain.)

PREPARATION

You'll need the following ingredients for your honey cakes:

● ¼ cup melted butter or margarine
● ¼ cup honey
● 2 cups Bisquick or other baking mix
● 1 teaspoon vanilla
● ½ teaspoon cinnamon
● ¼ cup milk.

You'll also need the following kitchen supplies:

● two bowls,
● a mixing spoon,
● measuring cups and spoons,
● a cookie sheet,
● potholders,
● an oven or toaster oven,
● small paper plates,
● and paper towels.

Ask:

- **How do you feel when you've complained?** (Grouchy; mad; not satisfied.)
- **How do you feel when you're thankful?** (Happy; peaceful; good.)
- **Would you rather complain or be thankful? Why?** (I'd rather be thankful because I'm happier that way; I'd rather be thankful, but I'll probably still complain if I don't like something.)

Say: **God wants us to be thankful for what we have and to trust him to provide for all our needs. God knows that's the way for us to be happy. This week, remember to be thankful and try not to complain.**

Toast Tablets

PREPARATION

You'll need:

- **slices of bread,**
- **honey,**
- **paper plates,**
- **plastic spoons and knives,**
- **paper towels,**
- **a cookie sheet,**
- **a potholder,**
- **and a toaster oven.**

STORY

The Ten Commandments (Exodus 19:9–20:21)

Moses received 10 special laws for God's people to live by. These laws, engraved on tablets of stone, showed God's people how to treat God and others. Use this story to encourage children to follow God's rules.

THE EXPERIENCE

Ask:

- **What are some rules we have in our classroom?**
- **What are some laws we have in our country?** (Don't kill anybody; don't rob a bank; people get to vote for the president.)
- **Why are there laws?** (To keep people from hurting each other; to keep us out of trouble.)

Say: **Our government makes laws to keep us safe. Today we're going to hear about ten laws God gave to his people.**

Tell the story of the Ten Commandments, found in Exodus 19:9–20:21.

Say: **Let's make some toast tablets to remind us of the stone tablets Moses received from God.**

Give children each a slice of bread to place on the cookie sheet. Toast the bread until it is golden. Transfer the toast to paper plates and give a plate to each child. Distribute plastic knives and have children cut their toast in half vertically. Then have them dip spoons in the honey and drizzle it over their toast halves to resemble writing. As they eat their toast tablets, ask:

- **What would life be like if we had no laws?** (Fun, we could do whatever we wanted; scary because we couldn't put criminals in jail.)
- **What are some rules we have to follow?** (I have to obey my parents; we have to obey the laws of the United States.)

Say: **God wants us to choose to do what's right. Remembering the ten laws God gave his people can help us do that.**

Communion Cup Print

STORY

Twelve spies go into Canaan (Numbers 13:1–14:25)

When Moses sent spies into Canaan, they brought back pomegranates, figs, grapes, and discouraging reports. God's people were so worried by these reports that they refused to try to take the land. This story will teach children not to let their worries keep them from trusting God.

THE EXPERIENCE

Ask:
● **What kind of grapes do you like to eat?**
Say: **We're going to make a grape-cluster print. Then we'll hear a story about some people who gathered a big bunch of grapes.**

Give children each a sheet of construction paper and one communion cup. Set out the recycled meat trays and lightly coat the center of each tray with purple paint. Have children turn their cups upside down, press them into the paint, and then press them onto the paper in a cluster design.

Tell the story of the spies sent into Canaan, found in Numbers 13:1–14:25.

Ask:
● **Why were God's people worried?** (Because they didn't know what they'd find in a new land; they were afraid they'd lose the battle.)
● **What did they decide to do?** (Complain; try to go back to Egypt; pick a new leader.)
● **What do you worry about?** (Bullies; getting good grades; that my parents might get a divorce.)
● **Does worrying help anything? Why or why not?** (No, worrying can't change anything; no, worrying sometimes makes me even more nervous; yes, if I'm worried about something I try to make it better.)
● **What can we do to help us not to worry?** (Trust God; pray; read the Bible; think of good things that might happen.)
Say: **God's people were so worried, they refused to go into his promised land. God wants us to trust him so we won't have to worry.**

Close in prayer, asking God to help children trust him when they feel worried this week.

PREPARATION

You'll need:

● plastic communion cups (available from various Christian supply companies),
● recycled plastic foam meat trays,
● light-colored construction paper,
● purple tempera paint,
● and paper towels.

Paper-Cup Donkeys

PREPARATION

You'll need:

- **one paper cup for each child,**
- **brown construction paper,**
- **poster board or heavy paper,**
- **scissors,**
- **tape,**
- **and permanent markers.**
- **Before class, cut ear patterns from poster board. Use the "Donkey Ear Pattern" below as a guide.**

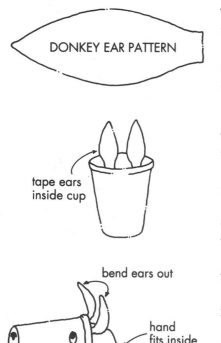

DONKEY EAR PATTERN

tape ears inside cup

bend ears out

hand fits inside

arm becomes donkey's neck

STORY

Balaam's talking donkey (Numbers 22:1-38)

When Balaam was hired by the king of Moab to curse God's people, God instructed Balaam to say only what God wanted him to say. Use Balaam's example to teach children ways they can honor God with their words.

THE EXPERIENCE

Ask:

- **How do animals communicate with people?** (Barking; wagging their tails; licking people's hands and faces.)
- **What kinds of animals can be taught to talk?**

Say: **We're going to hear a story today about a donkey who communicated with his master in a surprising way. But first we'll make paper cup donkeys so we can act out the story.**

Give children each a sheet of brown construction paper and show them how to trace and cut out two donkey ears. Distribute cups and demonstrate how to tape the ears inside the cup, then bend them out. Have children draw eyes on the sides of the cup and a mouth on the end. Then show them how to put the cups on their hands, using their arms as the donkey's neck.

Tell the story of Balaam, found in Numbers 22:1-38. As you tell the story, have the children use their donkeys to act out the donkey's actions.

Ask:

- **How did Balaam treat his donkey? Why?** (He kept hitting it with a stick to make it keep going; he was mean to it because he didn't understand why it kept stopping.)
- **How did God show Balaam he should say what God wanted?** (God sent an angel; God made the donkey talk.)
- **Do you think how we speak and what we say is important to God? Why?** (God can hear what we're saying; God wants us to say things that are nice—not mean.)
- **How does God want us to speak?** (Truthfully; kindly; without talking back to your mom and dad.)

Form pairs and have children use their donkeys to tell a partner one important thing they learned from today's story.

Say: **Balaam found out that what he said was very important. Our words are important, too. Let's remember this week to think before we speak and to speak the way God wants us to speak.**

Hide the Spies

STORY

Spies go into Jericho (Joshua 2 and 6)

When Joshua sent spies into Jericho, Rahab hid them. In return, they promised to save Rahab and her family. After the walls of Jericho fell, the spies kept their promise. Use this story to encourage children to keep their promises, too.

THE EXPERIENCE

● **When you play Hide-and-Seek, do you like to be a hider or a finder? Why?**

● **What kinds of places make good places to hide?** (In a closet; under a bed; behind the shower curtain.)

Say: **Our story today is about two men who had to hide so they wouldn't be captured. Listen to hear where they hid.**

Tell the story of the spies who went into Jericho, found in Joshua 2 and 6. Ask:

● **How do you think the spies felt knowing they could count on Rahab?** (Relieved; good; happy.)

Say: **Let's play a hiding game that will remind us of this story.**

Form pairs. Give each pair two clothespins and have them draw eyes on them to represent the spies. Have partners agree on a secret code to mark their spies, such as a colored band, a shape, or a combination of their initials. Circulate among the children as they are working to make sure each code is different.

When children have finished making their spies, say: **Choose one partner to leave the room. While you're gone, we'll hide all the spies. You'll have to count on your partner to help you find them. Be sure to check your secret code to make sure you've found the right spies.**

Lead one group of children out of the room. Tell them to stay near the door so you'll be able to call them back when the spies are hidden. Help the other children hide the spies. Tell them that they may help their partners only by saying "hot" or "cold."

Bring the first group back into the room to look for their spies. When all children have found their spies, switch roles and have the other partners leave the room. After the second group has found the spies, have children set the spies aside.

Gather the children together and ask:

● **Was it easy or hard to find your spies? Why?** (Easy because my partner helped me; our secret code was easy to find; hard because I kept finding other people's spies.)

● **Knowing you could count on your partner made it easier to find your spies. Can you think of a time your friends or family**

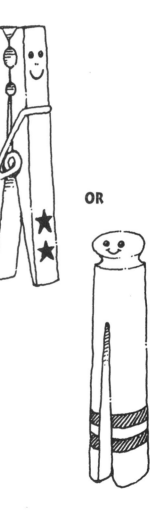

OR

knew they could count on you? Tell about it. (My mom counted on me to watch my little sister while she went outside; my friend counted on me to help him paint his bike.)

● **Have you ever thought you could count on someone, and then that person let you down? How did that make you feel?** (Like I wasn't important; sad; disappointed.)

● **Do you think it's important for people to be able to count on you?** (Yes, so people will believe me when I make promises; yes, so I won't disappoint other people.)

Say: **The spies knew they could count on Rahab. Rahab promised to help them hide, and she did. God wants us to be people others can count on. Choose one of the spies you made with your partner to take home. Write on the side of your spy one way others can count on you this week.**

Balloon Sunshine

- -

PREPARATION

You'll need:

● large paper plates,

● scissors,

● yellow crayons,

● 7-inch round yellow balloons,

● and markers.

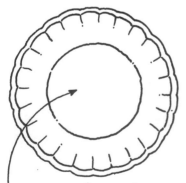

cut out center of paper plate

STORY

The sun stands still (Joshua 10:1-15)

When God's people fought the Amorites, Joshua told the sun and moon to stand still. God listened to Joshua and stopped the sun and moon. This story will teach children that God's power is strong enough to take care of any problem they might encounter.

THE EXPERIENCE

Ask:

● **When you look in the sky at night, what do you see?** (The moon; stars; sometimes I can see the Milky Way.)

● **Why can't we see the sun at night?** (It's too dark; the sun isn't out at night; the sun is shining on other parts of the world.)

● **When we say the sun is rising, what's really happening?** (The earth is turning; morning is coming.)

Say: **God made the sun to rise and set in the sky. We're going to hear a story now about a day God kept the sun from setting.**

Tell the story of the sun standing still found in Joshua 10:1-15.

Ask:

● **What problem was Joshua having the day he asked the sun to stand still?** (He was fighting the enemies; he was worried it would get dark and the people wouldn't be able to fight anymore.)

● **How did Joshua's problem get solved?** (Joshua asked God to help; God made the sun stand still.)

Say: **God helped Joshua win the battle by making the sun stand still. Let's make suns to remind us of this story.**

Give children each a paper plate and show them how to cut the center circle out of it. Demonstrate how to cut flares around the edge of the plate. Have children color their flares yellow.

Form pairs. Give children each a yellow balloon. Have one partner blow up a balloon until it's almost the size of the hole in the plate. Have the second partner hold the rim of the plate around the balloon as the balloon is being inflated until the "flares" are snug around it. Then have partners trade roles to inflate the second balloon and insert it into the hole in the plate. Children may need help tying the ends of their balloons.

Ask:

● **Do you think you could have created your balloon-sun by yourself? Why or why not?** (No, I couldn't blow up the balloon and hold the plate at the same time; yes, but it would have taken a lot longer.)

● **How did your partner help you create your sun?** (By holding the balloon; by blowing up the balloon; by telling me when to stop blowing up the balloon.)

Say: **Working with a partner made creating our suns a lot easier. In our story, God was Joshua's partner in battle. He helped Joshua solve his problem by keeping the sun from setting. If God can make the sun stand still, God can handle our problems.**

Close by completing the following sentence prayer with the children: When I trust God with my problems, I feel... Distribute markers and have children write their responses on their balloon-suns, then take turns reading them aloud. Say "Amen" after all children have shared.

cut edge to make flares

blow up yellow balloon to fit snugly inside

Against the Odds

STORY

Gideon (Judges 6–7)

Because Gideon trusted God, God gave him the courage to lead a small group of men against a mighty army. Use this story to teach children that God can give them courage to do hard things.

THE EXPERIENCE

Ask:

● **What is courage?** (Being brave; not being afraid.)

● **Tell about a time you did something that took courage.**

Say: **We're going to play a game today that might take a bit of courage.**

Form two teams. Have one team hold hands and form a line across the center of the room. Set the bowl of treats behind the line. Ask the other team:

● **Do you think you can get past this team to get the bowl of treats?**

Let the children respond, then direct two or three children to join the team that's holding hands. Ask:

● **Now do you think you can get past this team?**

Continue moving children onto the team that's holding hands until you have one child left. Say: **Your job is to get past this team. I'll give you a minute to think of how you'll do it. The other team will use the minute to think of how they can stop you.**

Give the child one or two suggestions for getting by the other team. Then encourage the other team to huddle together. Join the huddle and instruct them that when you say "go," they must re-form their line and stand two steps apart with their hands behind their backs and their eyes closed.

Have the team re-form their original line. Say: **When I say "go," try to get past this team. Go!**

Escort the child through the line to the treats. Encourage him or her to share the treats with the other children. As children are enjoying the treats, ask:

● **Before you knew about my instructions, did you think one person could get past a whole line of people? Why or why not?** (No, the people could just surround him or her; yes, if the one person tried enough times.)

Say: **Our story today is about a man who took a small army to fight a big army. Listen to hear how he succeeded.**

Tell the story of Gideon found in Judges 6–7.

Ask:

● **How did God's small army win against the enemy's big army?** (They blew their trumpets; they did what God said to do; they worked together.)

● **How do you think Gideon felt when God told him to leave part of his men behind?** (Confused; scared; worried that he would lose the battle.)

● **Why was Gideon able to have courage?** (He trusted God; he knew God would help him.)

● **How can you get courage?** (By trusting God; by praying; by asking a parent for help.)

Say: **Gideon was able to do something that took a lot of courage because he trusted God. If we trust God, we can do things that take a lot of courage, too.**

Samson Hair

STORY

Samson (Judges 13:1-5; 16:4-30)

God commanded Samson to never cut his hair. Samson's friend, Delilah, tempted him to reveal information that led Samson to disobey

God's command. When children hear about the trouble Samson's friend caused him, they'll be encouraged to choose their friends carefully.

THE EXPERIENCE

Ask:

● **How do you choose a friend?** (I do things with someone and start liking them; I choose friends who like the same things; I choose friends who live nearby.)

Say: **We're going to hear a story today about a man whose friend got him in trouble. This man's name was Samson, and he had very long hair. Let's make Samson hair now to wear while we listen to the story.**

Distribute construction paper and scissors. Show children how to cut a fringe by making several cuts in the paper from one long edge toward the other, stopping about an inch from the edge. Then help children curve the top edge of the fringe around to make a headband. Staple each child's headband to fit his or her head. Cut off any fringes that hang over the children's faces.

Tell the story of Samson and Delilah, found in Judges 13:1-5; 16:4-30. Let the children wear their Samson hair as you tell the story. As you're telling about Delilah cutting off Samson's hair, walk around and carefully cut the remaining fringes from the children's headbands.

Ask:

● **What kind of friend was Delilah?** (Bad; Samson couldn't trust her.)

● **Why did Samson lose his strength?** (He disobeyed God; he let Delilah cut his hair.)

● **Was obeying God important to Samson's friend, Delilah? How do you know?** (No, because she tried to get Samson to disobey; she cut Samson's hair even though she knew God told Samson to keep it long.)

● **Do you think Samson knew how Delilah felt about obeying God when he chose her as a friend? Why or why not?** (Yes, but he thought he could still obey God; no, if he knew she didn't obey God he wouldn't have asked her to be his friend.)

● **What are some qualities you look for in a friend?** (Nice; keeps promises; tells the truth.)

● **Why is it important to choose the right friends?** (The wrong friends can get you into trouble; to help you do right.)

Distribute markers and have kids write the qualities they'd look for in a friend on their headbands.

Say: **Samson got into trouble because he chose the wrong kind of friend. Good friends encourage us to do the right things and to follow God. The next time you're choosing a friend, remember the qualities you wrote on your headband and choose your friends wisely.**

PREPARATION

You'll need:

● large sheets of black or brown construction paper,

● a stapler,

● scissors,

● and markers.

cut on dotted lines to fringe

staple to fit like a headband

cut off fringe to make room for child's face

35

Grain Painting

PREPARATION

You'll need:

- a bag of unpopped popcorn,
- paper cups,
- plastic spoons,
- construction paper,
- tempera paint,
- large shallow boxes (like shirt boxes),
- and paper towels.

STORY

Ruth gathers grain (Ruth 1–2)

When Ruth went to Boaz's grain field to gather leftover grain, Boaz told his reapers to pull stalks of grain out of their bundles and leave them for Ruth to pick up. In this story children will see that everyone benefits from generosity.

THE EXPERIENCE

Ask:

- **Where have you seen grain growing?** (In a field; on a farm.)
- **What kinds of grains can you think of?** (Wheat; oats; corn.)
- **How do farmers harvest grain?** (With a tractor; with big machines.)

Say: **We're going to hear a story about a woman in the Bible who gathered grain in a farmer's field.**

Tell the story of Ruth gathering grain, found in Ruth 1–2.

Ask:

- **What is generosity?** (Giving; sharing; giving more than you have to.)
- **How was Boaz generous?** (He shared his grain with Ruth; he told his servants to leave extra grain.)

Say: **Now we're going to make a grain painting to remind us of this story by dipping popcorn in paint and shaking it in a box across a sheet of paper.**

Form four groups. Give one group all the popcorn, one group all the paper, one group all the boxes, and one group all the paint.

Say: **Using your supplies, make your grain paintings.**

If children complain that they don't have the supplies they need, encourage them to share supplies with other groups. Allow them a few minutes to think about this, then proceed with the activity.

Give children each a cup and a spoon. Help the popcorn group pour unpopped popcorn into cups until each cup is about ¼ full. Help the paint group add one spoonful of paint to each cup. Show children how to stir the paint into the corn kernels until the kernels are coated.

Help the paper group and the box group work together to place paper in each box. Reserve one box for used kernels. If you don't have enough boxes for all the children, have them take turns.

Show children how to pour the paint-coated kernels onto the paper and shake the box gently back and forth to create a design. Help children carefully remove their papers. Set the papers aside to dry and pour out the used kernels into the box you've reserved. Ask:

- **How did you feel when you discovered your group didn't have all the supplies you needed?** (Confused; mad; I wondered if you forgot to give us something.)

● **Could you have made your painting if the other groups hadn't shared their supplies with you? Explain.** (No, because I didn't have what I needed; yes, but it wouldn't have looked the same; I would have had to make something else.)

Say: **You've all shown generosity by sharing your supplies with each other. Have you ever known anyone who was generous? How did they show it?** (By sharing; by giving presents.)

● **How can you be generous at home or at school?** (Share my chips at lunch; ask a friend if he wants to use my basketball; give my brother something even if it's not his birthday.)

Say: **Boaz was generous to leave extra grain for Ruth. God blessed Boaz for his generosity. Whenever you see or eat grain, think of Boaz and remember to be generous.**

Big Ears

STORY

Samuel hears God (1 Samuel 3)

God called to young Samuel one night. Samuel listened, and God gave him a special message. Samuel's story encourages children to listen to the messages God gives them in his Word.

THE EXPERIENCE

Say: **Describe the ears of different animals. How are they different from your ears?**
● **Name some loud sounds you hear.** (Airplanes; motorcycles; hammering; thunder.)
● **Name some soft sounds you hear.** (Whispers; snow falling; crickets chirping.)

Say: **God has given us ears to hear all the wonderful sounds he's created. Today we're going to hear a story about a boy in the Bible who heard a sound in the night. But first, let's make some big ears to help us listen carefully to this story.**

Give each child a sheet of construction paper, a paper plate, crayons, and scissors. Show children how to draw around the paper plate to make a circle on the construction paper. Then have them cut out their circles and throw them away.

Have children draw one animal, human, or imaginary ear on each side of the circle. When children have finished drawing their ears, have them look through the circle to see how they look with those ears. Have the children trade papers to try on other ears.

Return ears to their original owners, then gather the class in a circle. Tell the story of God calling Samuel, found in 1 Samuel 3.

cut out circle

Ask:

● **How do you think Samuel felt when he realized God was calling him?** (Scared; amazed; excited.)

● **How can we hear God's messages?** (By reading the Bible; through teachers and parents; in our hearts.)

● **Why is it important to read God's Word?** (To know what God is like; to know what God wants us to do.)

● **What are some messages you know from God's Word?** (Be kind; obey parents; love others.)

Say: **Because Samuel was listening, he heard the important message God wanted to give him. God gives us important messages, too. We can read about them in God's Word. Wear your ears this week when you read the Bible and remember to listen carefully for God's message.**

Can You See Through This?

PREPARATION

You'll need:

● **one sheet of typing paper for each child,**

● **a strong flashlight,**

● **a book,**

● **different colors of construction paper,**

● **a clear plastic page protector,**

● **crayons,**

● **newspapers,**

● **cotton balls,**

● **and baby oil.**

STORY

David is anointed king (1 Samuel 16:1-13)

When Samuel was looking for a new king, he was surprised to find out that God had chosen David. David was just a little boy. He wasn't strong enough to fight great battles or wise enough to lead God's people. But God didn't choose David because of his strength or wisdom but because he loved God with his whole heart. This story will help children see that it's not outward appearance that's important but the attitude of a person's heart.

THE EXPERIENCE

Darken the room and let the children take turns trying to shine the light from the flashlight through the book, the different colors of construction paper, the typing paper, and the page protector.

Ask:

● **Which one of these things can you see through when you shine the flashlight on them?** (The page protector; maybe the typing paper.)

● **Why can't you see through the other things?** (The book is too thick; the construction paper is too heavy; the colors are too dark.)

Cover the work area with newspapers. Give children each a sheet of typing paper and crayons. Have them color a rainbow on the paper. Help children put baby oil on cotton balls and rub the oil over their rainbows.

Then let them shine the light through their papers again.

Ask:

● **What happened when you rubbed baby oil on your paper?** (I could see through it; the paper got slippery; the crayon smeared.)

Say: **God can see through us just like we can see through our rainbows. The Bible says that people may look at only our outside appearance, but God looks inside at our hearts. Let's hear a story now about how God looked at a young boy's heart.**

Tell the story of Samuel anointing David to be the king, found in 1 Samuel 16:1-13.

Ask:

● **Why is it important to not judge people by what they look like?** (You might think the wrong thing about them.)

● **How can we tell what's in a person's heart?** (By what they do; by what they say; sometimes I can't tell.)

Say: **Samuel learned that the most important thing to God is what's in a person's heart. Let's pray and thank God for looking at our hearts now.**

Dear God, thank you for not looking at us just on the outside. Help us to have loving, kind hearts that will make you proud. In Jesus' name, amen.

Shield of Faith

STORY

David and Goliath (1 Samuel 17)

Everyone in Israel's army was afraid to fight Goliath. Because he trusted God, young David challenged Goliath and knocked him to the ground with only a few stones and a slingshot. Like David, the children in your class can do great things with God's help.

THE EXPERIENCE

With the tape measure, let the children help you measure 9 feet, from the floor to the ceiling, or from one wall out into the room. Mark that spot with tape.

Tell the story of David and Goliath found in 1 Samuel 17. Refer to the 9-foot mark you've made to illustrate Goliath's height.

Ask:

● **What kind of equipment do you think a soldier in David's time usually carried into battle?** (A sword; a shield; a bow and arrow.)

● **What made David so brave?** (Faith in God; he killed lions and bears before.)

Say: **We can be brave like David with God's help. The Bible tells us about the armor God gives us.**

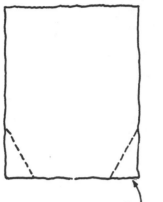

cut off corners
to make shield

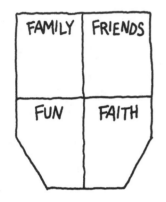

Read Ephesians 6:16. If you have older students in your class, ask a volunteer to read it.

Say: **Let's make a shield of faith to remind us of the armor God gives us for protection.**

Give children each half of a sheet of poster board and show them how to cut two corners off to make a shield shape. Distribute markers or crayons. Have children divide their shields into four sections and label the sections "Family," "Friends," "Fun," and "Faith." Have them decorate each section with drawings of important people or things from that part of their lives.

Ask:

● **Why is it important that we put our faith in God?** (God keeps his promises; God is powerful; God will take care of us.)

● **How did David show his faith in God?** (He went to fight Goliath; he wasn't afraid even though Goliath was much bigger than he was.)

● **How can we show our faith in God?** (By doing what God wants us to do; by telling other people about God; by praying.)

Say: **Because of David's faith in God, God used him to defeat Goliath and save his people. David's faith was his only shield. Our faith can be our shield, too.**

Braided Belt

PREPARATION

For each child, you'll need:

● **three strips of cloth 1 inch wide and 2 yards long.**

STORY

David and Jonathan (1 Samuel 18:1-4; 20:11-42)

Jonathan became David's best friend. Jonathan loved David so much he gave David his coat, armor, sword, bow, and belt. Use the example of Jonathan and David's friendship to teach children to be loving and faithful friends.

THE EXPERIENCE

Ask:

● **How many best friends do you have?**

● **What is the difference between a friend and a best friend?** (I only have one best friend; I tell secrets only to my best friend; I like my best friend more than my other friends.)

Say: **Our story today is about two best friends. Listen to hear what they did together.** Tell the story of David and Jonathan, found in 1 Samuel 18:1-4; 20:11-42.

Ask:

● **What else do you think David and Jonathan did together?** (Played games; fought battles; ate lunch.)

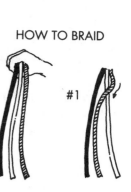

Say: **In our story, Jonathan gave David his belt. We're going to make our own braided belts, and we'll need to cooperate like friends do while we work.**

Form pairs. Give children each three strips of fabric. Have one child hold the ends of three of the strips. Show the other child how to braid the strips and then tie each end. Then have partners switch roles. When both partners have completed their braids, show the children how to tie the belts around their waists.

Ask:

● **How do friends treat each other?** (Friends help each other; friends stick up for each other.)

● **How can a person make friends?** (Be friendly; help others; smile.)

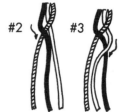

Form pairs. Read Proverbs 17:17. If you have older children in your class, ask a volunteer to read it. Say: **Friends are people who become part of our lives, just like these separate pieces of cloth became part of our belts. Tell your partner one thing you'll do to be a loving friend this week.**

Close in prayer, thanking God for the gift of friendship.

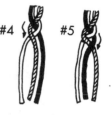

Abigail Snack

STORY

David and Abigail (1 Samuel 25:1-42)

David was angry. Although his men had protected Nabal's shepherds, Nabal would not share food with them. But Nabal's wife, Abigail, made peace, taking David the food he needed. Children often find themselves in situations where they're pressured to fight. Use Abigail's example to teach them to make peace instead of fighting.

THE EXPERIENCE

Preheat the oven to 350 degrees.

Ask:

● **How would you help two people who were arguing make peace with each other?** (Ask them to forgive each other; get an adult to help.)

Tell the story of David and Abigail found in 1 Samuel 25:1-42.

Say: **One of the foods Abigail took to David and his men was raisin cakes. We're going to make a kind of raisin cake.**

Have children wash their hands, then take turns helping with the following cooking jobs. Cream margarine and brown sugar together in one bowl. In the other bowl, mix the flour, baking powder, and salt. Then stir the flour mixture into the margarine mixture. Finally, stir in the oats.

Show children how to spray the baking pan with cooking oil spray.

PREPARATION

You'll need the following ingredients for your Abigail snack:

● 3 cups raisins
● 1½ cups margarine
● 2 cups brown sugar
● 3 cups flour
● 2 teaspoons baking powder
● ½ teaspoon salt
● and 3 cups quick oats.

PREPARATION

You'll also need the fol-
lowing kitchen supplies:

- cooking oil spray,
- an electric mixer,
- two mixing bowls,
- measuring cups and
  spoons,
- mixing spoons,
- a 9×13 baking pan,
- an oven,
- potholders,
- paper towels,
- and a knife.

Help them press half of the mixture into the pan and spread the raisins over it. Then help them spread the rest of the mixture on top.

Bake for 35 minutes. If you don't have an oven in your room, ask a teacher to take the pan to an oven and bring it back when it's done. If you have a short class time, bake another pan before class. Cut and serve on paper towels.

Ask:

- **How did Abigail make peace?** (She took food to David's men; she apologized.)
- **What are some ways we can make peace?** (Talk things out; apologize; do something nice for someone.)

Read Romans 12:18. If you have older children in your class, ask a volunteer to read the verse. Say: **Abigail found a way to make peace with David and his men. Let's remember to look for ways to make peace this week.**

English Muffin Owls

PREPARATION

You'll need the following ingredients for the English muffin owls:

- ½ English muffin for each child
- a jar of pizza sauce
- sliced black olives
- American cheese slices

You'll also need the following kitchen supplies:

- spoons,
- a cookie sheet,
- potholder,
- and an oven or broiler.

STORY

Solomon chooses wisdom (1 Kings 3:5-15)

When God offered to give Solomon whatever he wanted, Solomon asked for wisdom. Because God was pleased with Solomon's choice, he gave Solomon riches and honor as well as wisdom. Use Solomon's story to encourage children to make wise choices every day.

THE EXPERIENCE

Ask:

- **Have you ever seen an owl? Where?**
- **Some people say owls are wise. Are owls really wise?**
- **We're going to make a wise owl snack. While we eat our snacks, we'll hear a story about a very wise man.**

Have children wash their hands. Give children each half an English muffin and a spoon and have them take turns spreading pizza sauce on their muffins. As they spread the sauce, ask:

- **Who is someone you know that is wise?** (My teacher at school; my grandma.)
- **How can you tell those people are wise?** (They give good advice; they can figure out problems; they're patient; they listen.)

Give children each two black olive slices and a slice of American cheese. Show them how to make cheese triangles by folding their slices from corner to corner. Demonstrate how to place the cheese and olives on the muffins to make a beak and eyes. Place the muffins on the cookie sheet and broil until the cheese is bubbly.

Tell the story of Solomon, found in 1 Kings 3:5-15, while the children are eating their muffins.

Say: **Solomon made a wise choice. What are some wise choices you can make?** (Do my homework; obey parents; be kind; read the Bible.)

Say: **When we make wise choices, God will reward us. When you have to make a choice, think of Solomon and remember to choose wisely.**

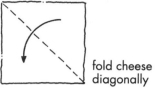

fold cheese diagonally

Origami Birds

STORY

Elijah is fed by birds (1 Kings 17:1-6)

When God sent a famine to the land, he continued to provide food for Elijah by sending ravens with bread and meat. Hearing Elijah's story will encourage children to notice and appreciate God's care for them.

THE EXPERIENCE

Ask:

● **What kinds of birds have you seen around your house?** (Sparrows; hummingbirds; blackbirds; I don't know.)

Say: **Our story today is about a man who was visited by ravens. Ravens are big, black birds.**

Tell the story of the ravens bringing food to Elijah found in 1 Kings 17:1-6.

Say: **We're going to make some birds to help us remember this story.**

Give children each a construction paper square. Be sure to keep one square for yourself. Slowly lead the children through the folds and cuts pictured, pausing after each one to make sure all children have completed it correctly. When children have finished their birds, ask:

● **How did God take care of Elijah?** (He sent birds; he provided food.)

● **How does God take care of you?** (Gives food and clothes; keeps us safe; gives us houses; gives us family and friends.)

Say: **God knew Elijah needed food. God knows what we need, too, and God will take care of us, just like he took care of Elijah. Let's remember to watch for the ways God takes care of us and thank God for his care.**

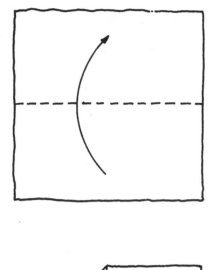 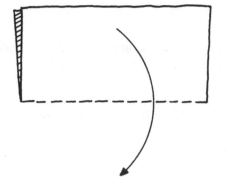 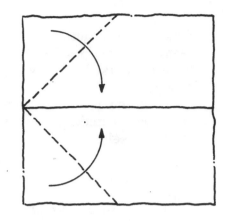

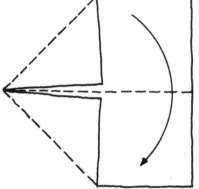 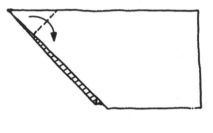 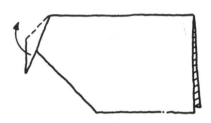

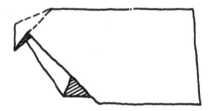 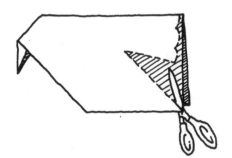 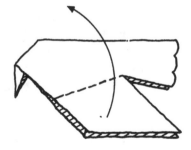

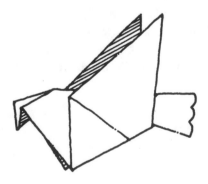

Reinforcer Altar

STORY

Elijah and the prophets of Baal (1 Kings 18:16-39)

Elijah challenged the prophets of Baal to see if their god would send fire to the altars they'd set up. The altar the prophets of Baal built never burned. Even though Elijah flooded his idol with water, God still set it on fire. Children may not fully understand the concept of idol worship, but they're not too young to learn to give God first place in their lives.

THE EXPERIENCE

Tell the story of Elijah and the prophets of Baal, found in 1 Kings 18:16-39.

Say: **Let's make altar pictures while we talk about this story.**

Give each child a sheet of construction paper. Set out the reinforcers and show children how to stick them on the paper to form an altar. Give children red, orange, and yellow crayons and have them color fire on their altars.

As children are working, ask:

● **Why did Elijah want the people to stop following Baal?** (Because Baal wasn't a real God; he wanted the people to obey God.)

● **How do you think you would have felt if you had been on Mount Carmel that day?** (Excited; scared; cheering for God.)

● **In our story, the Israelites followed Baal instead of following God. What are some things people today might love more than they love God?** (Sports; music; TV; friends; food.)

● **Why do we love and praise God more than everything and everyone else?** (God is the greatest; God made everything; God loves us all.)

Say: **God proved to the Israelites that he was greater than Baal. God is still greater than anything or anyone. Let's close our class today by giving three cheers for our great God. We'll say, "Hip, hip, hooray!" three times, then we'll say, "Yea, God!"**

Lead children in cheering for God.

color flames

stick on reinforcers to make altar

Paper-Cup Chariot

PREPARATION

For each child, you'll need:

- two paper fasteners,
- scissors,
- three paper cups,
- and markers.

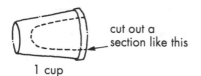

cut out a section like this

1 cup

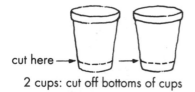

cut here →

2 cups: cut off bottoms of cups

attach cup bottoms to sides as wheels

STORY

Elijah goes into heaven (2 Kings 2:1-18)

When Elijah was carried to heaven in a fiery chariot, his friend and helper, Elisha, watched. Then Elisha became a prophet, following in Elijah's footsteps. Use Elisha's loyalty to Elijah to teach children to be loyal to their friends and families.

THE EXPERIENCE

Ask:

- **What would it be like to ride in a chariot?** (Kind of like riding in the back of a truck; it might be cold; the wind would blow your hair.)

Say: **We're going to make model chariots, and then we'll hear a story about a very unusual chariot.**

Give children each three paper cups, a pair of scissors, and two paper fasteners. Have them lay one cup on its side and cut out a section to create the body of their chariot. Show children how to cut out the bottom circles from two of the cups to create wheels for their chariots. Attach one circle to each side of the chariot with paper fasteners.

Tell the story of Elijah being taken to heaven in a chariot, found in 2 Kings 2:1-18.

Ask:

- **How did Elisha show he was a good friend to Elijah?** (He stayed with Elijah; he wanted to be like Elijah.)
- **What does being loyal mean?** (Being a friend no matter what happens; sticking up for your friends.)
- **Who are you loyal to?** (My family, my friends, my teachers.)
- **Why is it important to be loyal to friends and family?** (To encourage them; to let them know they can count on you.)

Say: **Because Elisha was loyal, God blessed him with Elijah's spirit and power. Write on your chariot the names of people you want to be loyal to. Let's remember to be loyal friends this week.**

Model House

STORY

Elisha is given a room on a roof (2 Kings 4:8-17)

A woman and her husband provided meals for Elisha when he passed through their town. They also built a room on their roof for him.

Children will learn from this story the importance of sharing what they have with others.

THE EXPERIENCE

Ask:

● **When guests come to your house, where do they stay?**

● **How do you feel about having company?**

Say: **We're going to hear a story today about a woman who wasn't expecting company. Listen to hear what she did.**

Tell the story of the woman and man who built a room on their roof for Elisha, found in 2 Kings 4:8-17.

Ask:

● **Why do you think these people shared their home with Elisha?** (They wanted to be friends; they knew he needed a place to stay; they wanted him to bless them.)

● **How do you think Elisha felt when the people shared?** (Happy; grateful; relieved to have a place to stay.)

● **How do you feel when someone shares with you?** (Glad; we both have more fun; it makes me want to share, too.)

Say: **We're going to build card houses. But we're going to have to share the work to get them done.**

Form pairs. Give one partner 12 large index cards and the other partner 12 small index cards. Have partners each draw the front door and windows of a house on two of their index cards.

Have children each tape four of their cards end to end, horizontally. Make sure they include the card with the doors and windows and lay it face down. Then have them tape two cards end to end, vertically. Have children tape their vertical cards to the top of the first card in their horizontal row.

Show children how to fold the four horizontal cards into a square, tape the "walls" together, then flip the vertical cards over to make a roof. Have them tape the roof to the walls. Then have children repeat the entire process with their other set of cards.

When children have each completed two houses, say: **Now put your small house on top of your large house to make a room on the roof like we heard about in our story.**

Children may exchange houses with one another with very little prompting. If any children protest that they don't have a small or large house, say: **Some of you have two small houses, and some of you have two large houses. If you trade one of your houses with your partner, you'll be able to put a room on the roof of your house.**

Give children a few moments to exchange houses and tape rooms to their roofs. Then ask:

● **When we were young we learned to share our toys. What are other things we can share?** (Food; our house; money.)

● **How can we share our time with others?** (By visiting with sick or old people; by playing with little brothers and sisters; by helping others.)

Say: **Each time you see your house with the room on the roof, remember how you shared with your partner. Then find a way you can share something with a friend or a family member.**

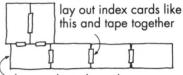

lay out index cards like this and tape together

door and windows drawn on other side of first card

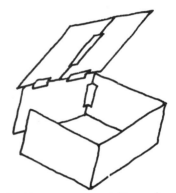

fold into square and flip roof cards down

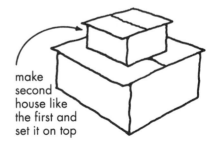

make second house like the first and set it on top

Dyeing Eggs

PREPARATION

You'll need:

- at least one boiled egg for each child,
- food color,
- crayons,
- a tablespoon,
- vinegar,
- paper bowls,
- spoons,
- water,
- and paper towels.

STORY

Naaman (2 Kings 5:1-14)

As a prophet, Elisha communicated God's instructions to the people. When Elisha told Naaman he would be healed if he dipped in the Jordan River, Naaman didn't understand, but he obeyed and was healed. The Bible communicates God's instructions to people today. Use this story to encourage children to do what the Bible says, even if they don't always understand.

THE EXPERIENCE

Ask:

- **Where do you like to go swimming?**
- **Did you ever swim in a river? If so, what was it like?** (It was really cold; it was kind of muddy; I saw a fish.)

Say: **We're going to hear a story today about a man who dipped in the Jordan River.**

Tell the story of Naaman, found in 2 Kings 5:1-14.

Ask:

- **Why do you think Naaman didn't want to dip in the Jordan River?** (Maybe it was dirty; too cold; it was too far away.)
- **What made Naaman change his mind?** (His friends; he thought about it some more.)

Say: **We're going to dip some eggs to remind us of Naaman's dips in the river.**

Put water in each bowl. Have several children drip food color in the bowls. Have other children add a tablespoon of vinegar to each bowl. Distribute boiled eggs and crayons. Have children write "Obey God" on their eggs. Then help them each place their egg on a spoon and dip it into the colored water seven times. Then let the eggs dry on paper towels.

Ask:

- **Why did Naaman think Elisha could heal him?** (He heard about Elisha from his wife's servant; he knew Elisha was a prophet.)
- **If you were sick, do you think you'd get well by washing yourself in the bathtub seven times? Why or why not?** (No, because the bathtub's not a river; stuff like that only happened in Bible times.)
- **Which do you think healed Naaman: the river water or God's power? Why?** (God's power, because if it was just the river water he could have washed in any river; the river water, because Elisha told him to wash in a certain river.)

Say: **Naaman was healed because he followed the directions of God's prophet. We can find out God's directions today by reading the Bible. We may not always understand why the Bible says** something, but we know God's directions will help us do what's right. Now my directions for you are to have fun peeling and eating your eggs!

Scroll Rolls

STORY

Josiah (2 Kings 22)

When King Josiah heard that the Book of the Teachings had been discovered in the temple, he studied it and helped his country turn back to God. Use this story to teach children that reading the Bible can help them follow God.

THE EXPERIENCE

Ask:

● **What would you do if you found something that had been lost for a long time?**

Say: **Our story today is about people who found something in the temple that had been lost for a long time.**

Tell the story of Josiah, found in 2 Kings 22.

Ask:

● **What did books look like in Bible times?** (They were rolled into scrolls; they didn't have pages or covers.)

● **Why didn't everyone have a Book of the Teachings at home?** (Books had to be written by hand; some people couldn't read.)

Say: **Since the Book of the Teachings was a scroll, today we're going to make scroll rolls.**

Have children wash their hands. Preheat the oven to the temperature suggested on the package of crescent roll dough. Give each child a paper plate to work on and a rectangular section of dough (two triangular sections together). Help children roll the rectangle from both ends to make a scroll, then place their scroll rolls on the cookie sheet. Bake the rolls for the time suggested on the package. If you don't have an oven in your room, ask a teacher or a helper to take the pan to an oven and bring it back when it's done.

While you're waiting for the scroll rolls to bake, ask:

● **What happened when the people forgot about the Book of the Teachings?** (They forgot how God wanted them to live; they didn't know what God wanted them to do.)

● **What happens when people forget to read the Bible?** (They forget about God; they do bad things.)

Say: **When God's people found the Book of the Teachings, they read it right away. It's important for us to read God's Word, too. The Bible reminds us of how God wants us to live.**

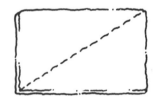

give each child a section like this

child rolls it like this

Many people follow a plan to help them read their Bibles every day. What kind of plan could you follow? When is the best time of the day for you to read your Bible?

Let's remember to read our Bibles every day.

Distribute the scroll rolls to the children. Let the children eat their rolls or take them home as a reminder to read their Bibles.

Self-Control Trail Mix

PREPARATION

You'll need:

- paper cups,
- a large bowl,
- peanuts,
- raisins,
- butterscotch chips,
- and coconut.

STORY

Daniel refuses the king's food (Daniel 1)

Even though they were offered the king's best food, Daniel and his friends would eat only vegetables and drink only water. God blessed them for eating foods they knew were healthy and pleasing to God. When children hear about Daniel's self-control, they'll be encouraged to practice self-control, too.

THE EXPERIENCE

Ask:

- **What are your favorite foods?**
- **What kinds of foods are we supposed to eat every day to be healthy?** (Vegetables; meat; fruit; bread.)
- **What kinds of foods should we only eat a little of?** (Dessert; gum; soda; things with a lot of sugar and fat.)

Say: **We're going to choose what foods to put into our snack, and then we'll hear a Bible story about four young men and what they chose to eat.**

Show children the butterscotch chips, raisins, peanuts, and coconut you have brought. Say: **I'd like you to help me decide which of these foods we should put into our trail mix to make a healthy and tasty snack.**

Hold up the foods, one at a time, and ask children how much of each they'd like to add to the trail mix. Encourage them to include plenty of healthy ingredients. Have children take turns adding ingredients to the bowl, stirring, and distributing the mix in paper cups. As children enjoy their trail mix, tell the story of Daniel and the king's food found in Daniel 1.

Ask:

- **Do you think Daniel thought about how good the king's food might look and taste?**
- **Why did Daniel refuse to eat the king's food?** (He knew there were certain foods God didn't want his people to eat; he didn't know what the king would serve.)
- **What do you do when you are tempted to eat food you know**

you shouldn't eat? (Not look at it; eat something else; stay out of the kitchen.)

● **What is self-control?** (Making yourself do what you know you should do; keeping yourself from doing what you know you shouldn't do.)

● **How did Daniel show self-control?** (He refused the king's food.)

● **Can you think of other times you might need self-control?** (When you're angry; when you want to buy things.)

Form pairs. Say: **Daniel used self-control to eat the right foods. There are many ways we can use self-control. Tell your partner one way you'll use self-control this week.**

Shield Tag

STORY

The fiery furnace (Daniel 3)

When Shadrach, Meshach, and Abednego refused to worship the king of Babylon, they were thrown into a furnace. Because they chose to worship God, God protected them from the fire. When children choose right actions that honor God, God will watch over them, too.

PREPARATION

You'll need:

● **a box of wadded-up newspapers.**

THE EXPERIENCE

Form a circle. Stand in the center of the circle and say: **We're going to play a game that's kind of like Dodge Ball. One person will stand in the center, and the rest of us will try to tag that person with newspapers. If you're tagged, you must pick someone to take your place in the center, then leave the game. I'll stand in the center first.**

Pass around the box of newspapers, then give students a cue to begin throwing them at you. Play the game a few times, then say: **Let's change the rules of this game. The person in the center may now choose four other people to act as human shields. The people standing in the circle still have to try to tag the center person, but the human shields can catch the newspapers and throw them back or hit them out of the way.**

If the center person hasn't been tagged after a minute, appoint a new person. After you've played the game a few times, have children help you pick up the newspapers. Then ask:

● **How did you feel when you were standing in the center all alone?** (Scared; I knew I'd get tagged; like I couldn't escape.)

● **How did you feel when you had human shields protecting you?** (Safe; like nobody could tag me; strong.)

Say: **Our story today is about three men who were shielded by God's protection.**

Tell the story of the fiery furnace, found in Daniel 3.

Ask:

● **Why do you think God protected Shadrach, Meshach, and Abednego?** (Because they didn't worship the statue; because they prayed; because they believed in God.)

● **Do you think it was easy for Shadrach, Meshach, and Abednego to do what was right? Why or why not?** (No, because they knew they might die; they didn't know for sure that God would save them; yes, they trusted God to take care of them, no matter what happened.)

● **Is it easy for you to do what's right? Why or why not?** (No, sometimes people at school make fun of me; yes, I know God wants me to do the right thing.)

● **Do you think God will protect you if you do what's right? Why or why not?**

Read Psalm 16:1. If you have older children in your class, ask a volunteer to read it. Say: **If we trust in God and do what's right, God will protect us just as he protected Shadrach, Meshach, and Abednego. Let's pray those Bible words together and ask God to protect us.**

Lead children in praying Psalm 16:1 together: **"Protect me, God, because I trust in you."**

Corncake Lions

STORY

Daniel in the lions' den (Daniel 6)

Daniel was thrown into a den of lions by a king because he prayed to God. But God closed the lions' mouths, Daniel was rescued, and the king praised God. Use Daniel's example to teach children the importance of prayer.

THE EXPERIENCE

Ask:

● **What's your favorite animal at the zoo?**
● **Which animals do you think are gentle?**
● **Which animals do you think are wild?**

Say: **We're going to make some corncake lions. Then we'll hear a story about these big, wild animals.**

Have children wash their hands. Help them mix the egg, sugar, baking powder, and salt in the bowl. Then add the flour and the milk. Help them mix in the cornmeal until the batter is as thick as pancake batter.

Have children watch as you pour several circles of batter into the

PREPARATION

You'll need the following ingredients for your corncake lions:

● **1 egg**
● **1 teaspoon sugar**
● **2 teaspoons baking powder**
● **1 teaspoon salt**
● **¼ cup flour**
● **1 cup milk**
● **cornmeal**
● **raisins**

draw batter out with a spoon as it cooks

place raisins on as eyes and nose

skillet. With a spoon, gently draw out the batter from the center of each circle to make spikes like a mane. Help children put raisins on the corncakes for the lions' eyes and nose before you turn them over. Place the finished corncakes on plates, and give one to each child.

While children are eating, tell the story of Daniel in the lions' den, found in Daniel 6. Ask:

● **Do you think you would pray, even if someone threatened to throw you in a lions' den?**

● **Why does God want us to pray?** (So we'll trust God; God likes us to talk to him.)

● **What do you talk to God about when you pray?** (I thank God for things; I ask God for things; I tell God how great he is.)

Form pairs. Say: **Prayer was so important to Daniel that he wouldn't stop praying for any reason. God wants each of us to enjoy talking with him so much that we'll keep praying, no matter what happens. Tell your partner something you'd like him or her to pray for, then spend a moment talking to God about those things. You can pray out loud or quietly to yourself.**

Close the prayer time with a short sentence thanking God for listening to the children's prayers.

Building and Measuring

STORY

Rebuilding the walls of Jerusalem (Nehemiah 2:11-20; 4:1-25; 6:1-9,15-16)

Nehemiah led God's people in rebuilding the walls of Jerusalem. In spite of discouraging interruptions, Nehemiah stayed at his task until it was completed. Use Nehemiah's example to encourage children to complete difficult tasks they may face.

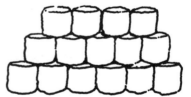

place marshmallows on each other like bricks

THE EXPERIENCE

Ask:

● **Have you ever seen a road construction crew building a wall next to the freeway? What do they build it with?**

Say: **Our story today is about a group of people who worked together to build a wall around a city.**

Tell the story of Nehemiah and the rebuilding of the walls of Jerusalem, found in Nehemiah 2:11-20; 4:1-25; 6:1-9, 15-16.

Ask:

PREPARATION

You'll need:

- newspapers,
- four bags of large marshmallows,
- two cans of white cake frosting,
- plastic knives and bowls,
- paper towels,
- tape measures or rulers,
- and a sheet of poster board.
- Cut the poster board lengthwise into four 5½-inch wide strips.
- Before class, divide the frosting into four bowls.

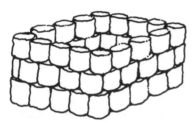

- **What happened to discourage Nehemiah?** (Enemies tried to attack the people; enemies sent around false reports.)
- **What did Nehemiah do?** (Prayed; kept building the wall.)

Say: **We're going to build a wall.**

Help children cover the tables with newspaper. Form four groups and number the groups from 1 to 4. Tell the children that each group will build a wall. Groups 1 and 3 will build the north and south walls. Groups 2 and 4 will build the east and west walls.

Give each group one strip of poster board to use as a base and one bag of marshmallows. Set out the frosting and distribute plastic knives. Show children how to spread frosting on the tops of the marshmallows and stack them like bricks to make the walls. Help children measure their walls as they build so all the walls are the same length and height. When all groups have finished, put all four walls together to make a fortress.

Ask:

- **What was hard about building your walls?** (Making sure they were all the same; the marshmallows kept falling off; spreading the frosting.)
- **How are your walls like the walls Nehemiah built?** (We had to work together; we had to do some things that were hard, but we kept working.)
- **What are some other difficult jobs you've had to do?** (Rake leaves; mow the lawn; help paint the house.)
- **What are some things you can do to help yourself finish a job when you're discouraged?** (Get someone to help; pray; remember Nehemiah.)

Say: **Even though discouraging things kept happening, Nehemiah kept working until he finished his job. God gave him the strength to keep going. God can give us the strength to complete difficult tasks, too.**

Cheese Fries

PREPARATION

You'll need:

- frozen french fries,
- a cookie sheet,
- paper towels,
- grated cheese,
- paper plates,
- an oven,
- a broiler,
- and a potholder.

STORY

Jonah (Jonah 1–3)

When Jonah first heard God's command to preach to the people of Nineveh, he ran away. But after he was thrown overboard and swallowed by a big fish, Jonah decided to obey. Use Jonah's example to help children learn the importance of choosing to obey God.

THE EXPERIENCE

Ask:

- **Tell about a time you helped your mom or dad cook. What did you cook?**

● **How did you know how to make the thing you were cooking?** (My mom helped me; we looked in the cookbook.)

● **Why is it important to follow directions when you're cooking something?** (So you can get it right; so you don't forget any ingredients; so you don't burn it.)

Say: **We're going to follow some cooking directions as closely as we can. The directions will tell us how to make cheese fries. While we're making them, we'll hear a story about a man who didn't follow directions but then changed his mind.**

Explain to the children that you're going to give each instruction only once. Wait for children to complete each instruction before giving the next one. Let the children be responsible for listening and following the directions. If you don't have an oven in your room, have an older child or teacher go to the oven to turn it on, bake, and remove the fries.

Set out the ingredients and cooking tools, then say: **These are the instructions. Wash your hands. Set the oven to the baking temperature listed on the package of fries. Place the frozen fries in a single layer on the cookie sheet. Put the cookie sheet in the oven. Set the timer for the time listed on the package directions.**

As the fries are baking, tell the story of Jonah, found in Jonah 1–3.

Ask:

● **Why was it important for Jonah to obey God?** (So the people of Nineveh could hear about God; so the people of Nineveh wouldn't be destroyed.)

● **What happened when Jonah didn't follow God's directions?** (He got thrown overboard; a big fish swallowed him; God knew Jonah ran away.)

● **What happens when we don't follow God's directions in the Bible?** (We get in trouble; we're not happy; we forget about God.)

● **Why is it important for us to follow God's directions?** (To show God we trust him; because God knows what's best for us.)

Say: **Jonah got into trouble when he didn't follow God's directions. Let's try to stay out of trouble by following God's directions.**

After the fries have been baked and returned to the room, put them on paper plates and pass them out to the children. Say: **Sprinkle the cheese on top of the fries. Broil the fries for just a few minutes until the cheese bubbles and browns.**

When the child or teacher returns with the fries, say: **Eat the cheese fries.**

As the children are enjoying their fries, have them talk with a partner about one or two ways they can follow God's directions this week.

New Testament

Popcorn Name

STORY

The birth of John the Baptist (Luke 1:5-25, 57-66)

Zechariah didn't believe his wife, Elizabeth, could have a child in her old age. As a result of his disbelief, God took away Zechariah's speech. When Zechariah and Elizabeth named their son "John," as God requested, Zechariah's voice returned. When children learn that God often chose significant names for people, they'll be encouraged to value their names and look for significance in them.

THE EXPERIENCE

Tell the story of the birth of John the Baptist, found in Luke 1:5-25, 57-66.

Ask:

● **How do parents choose a name for a baby when it's born?** (They choose a name they like; they name the baby after someone.)

● **Why do you think God told Zechariah and Elizabeth to name their son "John"?** (God wanted to help name the baby; God wanted to see if Zechariah would follow his directions.)

Say: **God sometimes gave Bible people special names. He changed Abram's name to "Abraham," which means "father of many." He changed Sarai's name to "Sarah," which means "princess." Let's find out what our names mean.**

Have children wash their hands. Help them pop the popcorn, then give children each a sheet of paper and glue. Have children write their names with glue in large letters across the paper, then stick the popped popcorn onto the glue. Help children look up their names in the name book. Write the meaning of each child's name at the bottom of his or her paper.

Ask:

● **What is your whole name?**

● **Why do you think your parents chose that name for you?** (I was named after my grandpa; they just liked the name; it sounded good.)

● **Do you think God knows your name? What else does God know about you?** (How tall I am; the color of my eyes and hair; how many hairs are on my head; how I'm feeling; everything.)

Say: **The names God chose for people in the Bible show what God knew about them. The Bible says that God knows all about us. Our names are important because they tell something about who we are.**

Close in prayer, thanking God for knowing each child in your class.

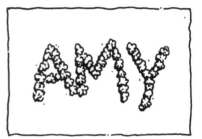

Who Brought the Message?

STORY

Gabriel announces Jesus' birth to Mary (Luke 1:26-38)

When the angel Gabriel announced to Mary that she'd be having a baby soon, she must have been shocked. But Mary believed God's messenger and rejoiced that God had chosen her to bring Jesus into the world. Children will learn to hear and obey God's message, just as Mary did.

THE EXPERIENCE

Ask:

● **What are some ways to send a message to someone?**

Say: **We're going to play "Who Brought the Message?" and then we'll hear a story about a messenger who brought a very unusual message.**

Choose three children to be "messengers." Have the messengers stand at the front of the room. Have the rest of the children sit on the floor, facing the back of the room. Have them cover their eyes with one hand and hold the other hand at shoulder height, palm up.

Say: **Each messenger will gently tap the hand of one person, then return to the front of the room. Then I'll ask you to open your eyes. If you were tapped by a messenger, I'll ask you to stand up and try to guess which messenger tapped you. You'll get one guess. If you guess the right messenger, you get to take his or her place in the next game. If you don't guess the right messenger, the messenger that tapped you gets to be a messenger again in the next game.**

Play the game several times, then say: **Mary never would have guessed she'd get a message from an angel. Let's find out about the message she received.**

Tell the story of Gabriel bringing the message to Mary, found in Luke 1:26-38.

Ask:

● **How would you feel if you were Mary?** (Amazed; surprised; scared; excited.)

● **Why do you think Mary agreed to do what the angel said?** (She didn't have much choice; she trusted God; she was happy to be chosen.)

● **God sent an angel to deliver a message to Mary. How do we get messages from God today?** (By reading the Bible; by praying; by coming to church.)

● **How do you feel when you read God's message in the Bible or hear about it at church?** (Glad to have the Bible; worried I won't be able to remember everything God wants me to do.)

Say: **Mary heard God's message and obeyed. We can obey God, too. We can read God's message in the Bible and then do what God wants us to do.**

Manger Cards

STORY

Jesus' birth (Luke 2:1-7)

God's promise to send a Messiah was fulfilled the night Jesus was born in a stable in Bethlehem. When children hear that God kept this promise, they'll be encouraged to believe God will keep all his promises.

THE EXPERIENCE

Invite children to help you tell the story of Jesus' birth, found in Luke 2:1-7. After you finish telling the story, say: **Now we'll make a manger picture while we talk about what this story means.**

Give children each a sheet of construction paper and have them fold the paper from both sides so the edges meet in the center. Show children how to make legs for their mangers by gluing two pretzel sticks to the center panel of their papers. Help children glue Spanish moss above the pretzel sticks to make hay for their mangers, then press one of their thumbs on the ink pad and make two thumbprints above the Spanish moss to represent the baby in the manger.

Say: **God promised to send baby Jesus long before he was born. Hundreds of years before Jesus was born, a prophet named Micah said, "But you, Bethlehem,... from you will come one who will rule Israel, for me. He comes from very old times, from days long ago" (Micah 5:2). Many other prophets also told of God's promise that Jesus would come. Jesus' birth means that God kept his promise.**

Ask:

● **What promises have you made and kept?** (I promised my mom I'd clean my room; I promised my friend I'd come over and play.)

● **What other promises has God made?** (To be with us always; to take care of us.)

● **Why do you think God keeps all his promises?** (So we'll trust him; because God loves us.)

Help children each write "God keeps his promises" on their cards in an arc over the manger.

Say: **God kept his promise and sent Jesus. When you look at your card, remember that God keeps all his promises. Let's**

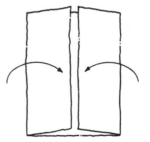

thank God for keeping his promises now. Dear God, thank you for sending Jesus and for keeping all your wonderful promises. In Jesus' name, Amen.

Graham Cracker Stable

PREPARATION

You'll need:

- graham crackers,
- miniature marshmallows,
- paper plates,
- copies of the "Nativity Cutouts" handout (p. 63),
- and frosting "glue."
- To make frosting glue, combine ½ pound powdered sugar, 2 egg whites, and ¼ teaspoon cream of tartar. Beat 7 to 10 minutes. Refrigerate in a tightly covered container.
- Cut out one set of nativity cutouts before class.

STORY

Shepherds visit baby Jesus (Luke 2:8-20)

When the shepherds heard about Jesus' birth, they hurried to find the baby in the stable. As they returned to their sheep, they praised God for what they had seen. Use the story of the shepherds to encourage children to praise God for Jesus' birth.

THE EXPERIENCE

Ask:

- **What's it like to look up into a starry sky at night?**
- **Imagine looking up into a sky filled with angels and God's glory. What do you think that would be like?** (Bright; shiny; beautiful; awesome.)

Tell the story of the angels and the shepherds found in Luke 2:8-20.

Say: **Let's make a model of what that stable might have looked like.**

Have children wash their hands. Set out the frosting glue and give children each a paper plate and three graham cracker squares. Show children how to dip the ends of their crackers in the frosting just enough to coat the edges. Then help them arrange their crackers in a triangular shape. Have children hold their crackers in place for one minute while the frosting sets.

Distribute miniature marshmallows and demonstrate how to draw faces and tails on the ends. Help children glue several marshmallow "sheep" to the floors of their stables. Then give children each a set of nativity cutouts. As children are cutting their nativity cutouts, demonstrate how to glue them in and around the stable using the sample cutouts you prepared before class. Set the stables aside to dry.

Ask:

- **What did the shepherds do after they saw baby Jesus?**
- **Why do you think the shepherds praised God?** (Because God kept his promise; they wanted to thank God for sending Jesus.)
- **What are some reasons we can praise God?** (God made us; God gives us things we need; God sent Jesus.)

63

frosting used for glue

Form a circle, then say: **Let's praise God right now. I'm going to start a sentence prayer, and each of you will get a chance to finish it. Here's the sentence: "God, you're really great because..."**

Continue repeating the prayer until each child in the circle has had a chance to contribute. Encourage children to take their stable scenes home to use as a praise center during the Christmas season.

Wise Men Cups

PREPARATION

You'll need:

● **scissors,**

● **crayons,**

● **and glue.**

You'll also need for each child:

● **one 14-ounce plastic foam cup**

● **and two 8½-ounce plastic foam cups.**

cut here
small cup #1

cut out large section of small cup #2

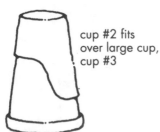

cup #2 fits over large cup, cup #3

STORY

Wise men visit baby Jesus (Matthew 2:1-12)

Wise men from the east followed a special star to find Jesus, the newborn king. When they found him, they bowed down and worshiped him and gave him precious gifts. Use this story to encourage children that they, too, can worship Jesus, the newborn king.

THE EXPERIENCE

Ask:

● **What do you think about when you see the stars?** (I try to count them; I think about how far away they are; I remember that God made them.)

Say: **We're going to make figures of some men who studied the stars, then we'll hear a story about them.**

Set out the crayons and glue. Give children each one large cup, two small cups, and a pair of scissors. Show them how to cut off the bottom rim of one of their small cups. Then help them cut out a large curved section from the other small cup as shown.

Help children turn their cups over and fit the small cup they've just cut over the large one. Have them color the small bottom rim section they've cut out to look like a crown, then glue their crowns on top of their stacked cups. Help children draw a wise man's face and beard on the small cup section and a robe on the large cup section. Show children how to turn the wise man's head from side to side by moving the small cup back and forth over the large one.

When children have finished their wise men, say: **The men in our story were very wise, and when they saw a bright star, they knew something special had happened. Listen to see what that special thing was.**

Tell the story of the wise men visiting baby Jesus, found in Matthew 2:1-12. As you tell the story, encourage children to move their wise men's heads as if they were looking for the baby Jesus.

Ask:

● **Why do you think the wise men worshiped baby Jesus?** (They knew he was a king; they were glad they'd found him.)

● **What are some ways we can worship today?** (Praying; singing; living the way God wants us to live.)

● **What can we give to Jesus?** (Praise; ourselves; the things we own; we could write a song or poem.)

Form pairs. Have children share with a partner one gift they'll give to Jesus this week. Close in prayer, thanking God for the gift of his son.

small rim from #1 colored to be crown

head rotates

draw wise man's face and head and color wise man's robe

The Carpenter's Shop

STORY

Jesus grows up (Luke 2:51-52; Matthew 13:55)

Joseph was a carpenter, and Jesus was known as the carpenter's son. Although Jesus was the son of God, he was willing to be a part of his earthly family. As a child, Jesus probably performed the normal household chores assigned to children of that day. Use this story to encourage children to take responsibility in their own families.

THE EXPERIENCE

Tell the story of Jesus growing up in Nazareth, found in Luke 2:51-52. You may also wish to include facts from Matthew 13:55.

Ask:

● **What does a carpenter do?** (Builds houses; hammers; makes things.)

Say: **Jesus' earthly father was a carpenter. To get an idea what it might have been like to live in Jesus' house, let's make a carpenter's shop.**

Cover a table with newspapers. Set out wood, hammers, nails, paints, and paintbrushes. Tell children they may build whatever they can imagine with the material and tools you've provided. Encourage them to help each other and to clean up their messes as they work. Circulate among the children to assist them as necessary. Let children talk about their creations. After they've cleaned up their mess, ask:

● **How do you think Jesus helped Joseph clean up the carpenter's shop?**

● **What responsibilities do you have at home?**

● **How do you feel when you do something that helps out your mom or dad?** (Good; proud; happy.)

Say: **Even though Jesus knew he was the son of God, he lived as a son to Mary and Joseph, and he obeyed them. Each one of us has certain responsibilities in our families, too. Let's remember to take care of our responsibilities with a happy heart so we can grow in favor with God and people, just like Jesus did.**

PREPARATION

You'll need:

● a variety of small wood scraps and blocks,

● hammers,

● nails,

● paint,

● paintbrushes,

● and newspapers.

● You may wish to ask an additional adult helper to assist in supervising the children as they work on their carpentry projects.

Starting Off Right

STORY

Jesus is baptized (Matthew 3:13-17)

Jesus asked John to baptize him because he wanted to start out his ministry right. Jesus started out right by obeying God. The children in your class can start out right by obeying, too.

THE EXPERIENCE

Display the celery sticks where students can see them. Hold up the jar of peanut butter and the tube of toothpaste.

Say: **I've brought some celery sticks for a snack today. Which one of these should we put on our celery sticks? Why?** (Peanut butter, because it tastes good; toothpaste is for brushing your teeth, not for eating.)

Say: **But I thought maybe we could do something good for our teeth and have a snack at the same time. Are you sure you don't want to try some toothpaste on your celery sticks? Let's take a vote. How many people think toothpaste would taste better on celery sticks? How many people think peanut butter would taste better on celery sticks?**

Have children vote by raising their hands. Have children each put several celery sticks and a spoonful of peanut butter onto their plates. Give them each a plastic knife and let them spread peanut butter on their celery.

As the children are eating, say: **You made the right choice by putting peanut butter on your celery sticks. Toothpaste would have been the wrong choice!**

Ask:

- **Can you think of times you have to choose between right and wrong?** (When a friend wants me to do something I'm not supposed to do; when I'm angry and I have to decide how to act.)

Say: **Jesus wanted to make all the right choices when he lived here on earth. Our story today is about a choice Jesus made.**

Tell the story of Jesus' baptism, found in Matthew 3:13-17.

Ask:

- **What reason did Jesus give for wanting to be baptized?** (To do what God wanted.)
- **Can you think of a time when you decided to do something because it was the right thing to do?**

Say: **Jesus chose to be baptized because it was the right thing to do. Sometimes we make decisions for that same reason. God wants us to choose to do right. Let's start off right by obeying God this week.**

Caterpillar to Butterfly

STORY

Jesus changes water into wine (John 2:1-11)

When the wedding host ran out of wine, Jesus changed water into wine. When children hear about the amazing change Jesus made at the wedding, they'll be encouraged to ask Jesus to change their hearts and lives.

THE EXPERIENCE

Ask:

● **What kinds of changes do you see happening in the world around us?** (Leaves changing colors; plants growing; water changing into ice; night changing into day.)

Say: **Our story today is about an amazing change Jesus made.**

Tell the story of Jesus changing water into wine, found in John 2:1-11.

Say: **To remind us of this story, we're going to make a picture of something from nature that makes an amazing change.**

Set out the crayons or markers and the tape. Give children each a sheet of construction paper, 10 or 12 hole reinforcers, a small paper plate, and scissors. Show children how to stick the reinforcers in a line on the paper to make a caterpillar. Then help them cut two wide wedges out of the paper plate. Have them color the wedges to make butterfly wings and tape the wings onto the caterpillar.

Ask:

● **When have you seen a caterpillar's cocoon? What was it like?**

● **The caterpillar makes an amazing change. What amazing change did Jesus make at the wedding? Why?** (To make more wine; to show how powerful he was; to amaze people.)

● **The caterpillar changes the way it looks on the outside. Do you think Jesus can change the way we look on the inside? Why?** (Yes, Jesus can change our hearts; Jesus can help us be nicer; we have to make changes ourselves.)

● **How do we get Jesus to change our hearts?** (We ask him.)

Say: **Jesus can make amazing changes. He changed water into wine. If we want him to, and ask him to, Jesus will change our hearts. Write on your caterpillar something you'd like Jesus to help you change this week.**

PREPARATION

You'll need:

● construction paper,
● hole reinforcers for notebook paper,
● small paper plates,
● scissors,
● crayons or markers,
● and tape.

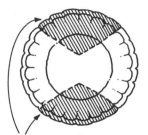

cut out two wide wedges
to make wings

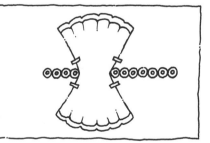

tape "wings" on

Tin Can Lanterns

PREPARATION

You'll need:

- an empty tin can
- and a votive candle for each child,
- hammers,
- nails,
- and matches.
- Before class, remove the labels from the cans and wash them. Then fill the cans with water and freeze them. The cans will be very cold. You may want to bring potholders for children to wrap around the cans as they hold them.

STORY

Nicodemus visits Jesus (John 3:1-21)

Nicodemus came to Jesus one night with questions. Jesus answered his questions and taught him. Children will learn from Nicodemus' example that God wants us to go to him to seek answers to our questions.

THE EXPERIENCE

Ask:

● **What can we use to help us see when it's dark?** (Candles; flashlights; lamps.)

Say: **We're going to make tin lanterns now. Then we'll hear a story about someone who went through the dark to find answers to his questions.**

Form pairs. Give each child a frozen tin can. Set out hammers, nails, and pot holders. Show children how to make designs in their tin cans by gently pounding nail holes. Have one partner hold the can with a pot holder while the other partner carefully pounds holes. Then have partners switch roles. You may need to help younger children with the hammering.

By the time children have finished, you should be able to remove the ice from the cans. If the ice hasn't melted, run the cans under hot water. Empty the cans, then set a votive candle in the bottom of each can to make a lantern. Light the lanterns, then have children arrange them on the table. Turn out the lights in the room and tell the story of Nicodemus, found in John 3:1-21.

Ask:

● **Why did Nicodemus come to see Jesus?** (He wanted to ask questions; he wanted to meet Jesus.)

● **Why do you think he came at night?** (Maybe he didn't want anyone to see him with Jesus; maybe he was too busy during the day.)

● **Where can you go when you're curious and you have questions?** (To parents; to teachers; to God.)

Say: **Nicodemus went to Jesus to find answers to his questions. We can go to Jesus, too. We can find out what Jesus said by reading the Bible. Each time you see your lantern, remember to look in the Bible for answers to your questions.**

Mirror Image

STORY

Jesus calls Peter, Andrew, James, and John (Mark 1:16-20)

Jesus first saw Peter, Andrew, James, and John when they were working as fishermen by the lake. He asked them to follow him, and they did. The children in your class can follow Jesus by trying to be more like him. Use this story to teach children what it means to follow Jesus.

THE EXPERIENCE

Ask:
● **What do people use to catch fish when they go fishing?** (Worms; bait; hooks; fishing flies; fishing poles.)
● **What do you think would be the most fun about fishing?**
Say: **We're going to hear a story now about four men who met Jesus while they were fishing.**

Tell the story of Jesus calling Peter, Andrew, James, and John, found in Mark 1:16-20.

Ask:
● **How did these fishermen follow Jesus?** (They left their fishing nets and went with him.)
● **Jesus wants us to follow him, too. Let's play a following game.**

Form pairs. Have partners stand facing each other. Choose one partner to be the leader and one partner to be the mirror. Have the mirror follow the leader's movements as closely as possible, so it looks like they're doing the movement together. Then have partners switch roles.

Children may enjoy watching each other do this activity. You may want to have pairs take turns so others can watch. Or you can let pairs work simultaneously and videotape the activity to show to the children.

Ask:
● **Was it easy or hard to be a mirror for your partner's movements? Why?** (Easy, because I just did whatever my partner did; hard, because my partner kept changing movements.)
● **What did you do to help yourself reflect those movements?** (I had to watch closely; I tried to think what my partner would do next.)
● **How can we reflect Jesus?** (By knowing what Jesus would do; by reading what Jesus did in the Bible.)
● **What does "following" Jesus mean?** (Going where Jesus wants us to go; doing what Jesus wants us to do.)
● **How can we know what Jesus wants us to do?** (By looking in the Bible; by praying; by watching for Jesus to guide us.)
Say: **Peter, Andrew, James, and John walked away from their boats and their nets and followed Jesus. Jesus wants us to follow**

him, too. The more we learn about Jesus, the more we'll be able to be a mirror of him, just like we were mirrors of our partners today.

Around Together

- - - - - - - - - - - - - - - - -

PREPARATION

You'll need:

- tape,
- scissors,
- and two rolls of streamers (different colors) cut into 6-foot lengths.
- For each group of nine or fewer children you'll need a broom or mop with a long handle.

STORY

Jesus chooses apostles (Luke 6:12-16)

Jesus chose 12 followers to be his closest co-workers as he taught and helped people. Jesus' followers must have had to work closely together as they traveled and ministered with Jesus. Use this story to teach children that they can work together, too.

THE EXPERIENCE

Ask:

● **Do you think it was easy or hard for Jesus' followers to work together? Explain.** (Easy because they just did what Jesus said; it would be hard for 12 people to work together.)

Say: **Jesus' followers had to work together all the time. Let's hear a story about them now.**

Tell the story of Jesus choosing 12 apostles, found in Luke 6:12-16. After the story, ask:

● **What did the 12 apostles do together?** (Travel; eat; listen to Jesus.)

● **What attitudes are good to have when you work with other people?** (Patience; cheerfulness; thankfulness.)

Say: **We're going to practice working together today. Remember those attitudes as we play our game.**

Form groups of no more than nine and have the groups form circles. Make sure each group has an uneven number of children. Designate one child to hold the broom or mop handle. Have that person stand in the center of the circle.

Give the other children streamers, alternating colors around the group. Help children each hold one end of their streamer and tape the other end to the top of the broom or mop handle. Have the person with the broom or mop hold the handle straight up in the air. Show the children with the first color how to walk around the circle clockwise. Have the children with the second color walk around counterclockwise at the same time.

Help children weave around each other as they walk, going to the left of the first person they meet, to the right of the next person, and so on. As the children walk around, the streamers will weave around the pole. If children have trouble catching on to this activity, you may want to practice it a few times without the streamers. Repeat the activity to give the children holding the mop or broom handle a chance to participate. Then ask:

● **Was it easy or hard to walk around the pole together? Why?** (Easy because I followed the directions; hard because I kept forgetting which way to go next; I kept bumping into people.)

● **We had to work together to weave our streamers around the pole today. Where are other places you'd need to work together with a group?** (On a team; in a choir; in a family.)

● **Is it easier to work with others or to work alone? Explain.** (It's easier to work with others because they help me; it's easier to work alone because sometimes I want to do things my own way.)

Say: **Jesus' followers had to cooperate with each other. They worked together. Let's follow their example and cooperate with each other when we have a group job to do.**

Flower Cookies

STORY

Jesus teaches about the lilies of the field (Matthew 6:25-34)

When he wanted to make a point about God's care, Jesus used birds and flowers as examples. If God takes care of birds and flowers, Jesus pointed out, God will take care of people. Jesus' teaching will encourage children to trust God to supply their needs.

THE EXPERIENCE

Ask:

● **What's your favorite flower?** (Roses; daisies; daffodils; dandelions.)

● **What's your favorite bird?** (Eagle; woodpecker; crow; pigeon; penguin.)

Say: **Today we'll hear a lesson Jesus taught about flowers and birds.**

Tell the story of Jesus teaching about the birds and flowers, found in Matthew 6:25-34.

Say: **We're going to make flower cookies to help us remember this story.**

Have children wash their hands. Heat the oven to the temperature recommended on the package of dough. Slice the dough into circles and give children each 1½ dough circles, a piece of foil, and a plastic knife. Demonstrate how to cut the whole circle and the half circle into six quarters.

Have children roll one of their dough quarters into a ball and place it on their foil, then place the other five quarters around it to make petals for their flowers. Pour food coloring into the cups. Demonstrate how to

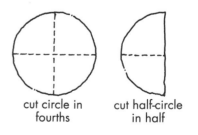

cut circle in fourths   cut half-circle in half

arrange like a flower

use cotton swabs to paint food coloring onto the flowers. Leave the flower cookies on the foil and place them on the cookie sheet.

Bake the cookies according to the instructions on the package. If you don't have an oven in your room, ask a teacher to take the cookies to an oven and return them when they're done.

As children are enjoying their cookies, ask:

● **Why do you think Jesus said not to worry?** (Jesus wanted us to be happy; Jesus knew God would take care of us.)

● **What is a worried person like?** (Grumpy; frowning; grouchy.)

● **Can you worry and be happy at the same time? Why or why not?**

● **What can we do when we're tempted to worry?** (Remember what Jesus said; pray; think about other things.)

Say: **Jesus told us not to worry, because God will give us what we need. If God clothes the flowers and feeds the birds, we can trust him to take care of us. Remember God's care the next time you see beautiful flowers outside.**

Do You Believe?

PREPARATION

You'll need:

● napkins

● and a bag of unshelled peanuts.

STORY

The centurion's servant (Luke 7:1-10)

The Roman centurion believed Jesus could heal his servant simply by speaking a word. And that's what happened. Children will learn from this story that faith sometimes means trusting things they can't see.

THE EXPERIENCE

Ask:

● **Do you believe I can give you something without touching it? How could I do it?** (You could wear gloves; you could pick it up with a spoon or other tool.)

● **Do you believe I can give you something no human hand has ever touched? Explain.** (No, lots of people probably touched it before you; maybe everyone who touched it wore gloves.)

Distribute napkins, then take several unshelled peanuts from the bag and offer them to the children. They will protest that you're touching the peanut. Carefully split one peanut's shell in half, and drop the peanuts inside onto a child's napkin.

Say: **Now do you believe I can give you something no human hand has ever touched?**

Give children each several shelled peanuts. Show them how to remove the shells, then say: **After you saw the peanuts, you believed I could give you something no human hand ever touched. While you're eating your peanuts, we'll hear a story about a man who** believed Jesus could heal his servant without even touching him.

Tell the story of the centurion's servant, found in Luke 7:1-10.

Ask:

● **Why didn't the centurion ask Jesus to come to his house to heal his servant?** (Because he knew Jesus could heal his servant without touching him; because he knew Jesus was busy.)

● **How do you think the servant felt when he was suddenly healed?** (Excited; confused; curious how he was healed; glad not to be sick anymore.)

● **Which is easier, believing something you've seen or believing something you haven't seen? Explain.** (Believing something you've seen, because if you see it, you know it happened; sometimes you can believe something you haven't seen if someone you trust tells you about it.)

Read Hebrews 11:1. If you have older children in your class, ask a volunteer to read it. Then say: **The centurion didn't need to see Jesus heal his servant to believe it. He knew Jesus was more powerful than his servant's sickness. Even though we can't see Jesus today, we still believe in him. Tell a partner one way you can show your faith in Jesus this week.**

Close in prayer, asking God to increase the children's faith.

Seeds

STORY

The sower and the seed (Luke 8:4-15)

Jesus told a story about a farmer planting seed. He said the seed was like the Word of God, and the different soils were like different kinds of people. When children hear this story, they'll be encouraged to open their hearts to God.

THE EXPERIENCE

Ask:

● **What kinds of plants do people grow in gardens?** (Flowers; vegetables; trees; bushes.)

● **What would you have to do to take care of a garden?** (Pull out the weeds; water the plants.)

Say: **We're going to look at the insides of seeds, and then we'll hear a story about the seed in a farmer's garden.**

Give each child a paper towel and one moistened seed from the pie pan. Show children how to pull the two halves of the seed apart. Pass around the magnifying glasses so children can examine the baby plants inside their seeds. Then give each child a clear plastic cup, two more paper towels, and three or four dried beans. Help children fold their paper towels and line their cups with them.

Show children how to place their beans between the cup and the paper towels, then moisten the paper towels with water. Encourage them to take their cups home, place them in sunlight, and keep the paper towels moist.

Tell the story of the sower and the seed, found in Luke 8:4-15.

Say: **God's Word is like the seeds we just planted. God wants to plant his Word in our hearts.**

Ask:

- **How can trouble cause people to turn away from God's Word?** (By making them think God isn't taking care of them; by making them think about the trouble instead of God.)
- **How can worries, riches and pleasure cause people to turn away from God's Word?** (By making them think about those things instead of God; by trusting money instead of God.)
- **How can we keep God's Word in our hearts?** (By reading God's Word often; by praying; by memorizing Bible verses.)

Say: **The seed planted in good soil made a crop 100 times more than what was planted. When we keep God's Word in our hearts, God can do wonderful things in our lives. Let's be good soil and welcome God's Word into our hearts!**

Storm in a Jar

STORY

Jesus stills the storm (Mark 4:35-41)

Jesus slept as he and his disciples sailed across the lake. When a storm blew in, the disciples woke Jesus, and he calmed the storm. This story will encourage children to trust Jesus when they're afraid.

THE EXPERIENCE

Ask:

- **What are some different kinds of storms?** (Tornadoes; hurricanes; blizzards; thunderstorms.)
- **What kinds of storms have you been in?**

Say: **Listen to this story to hear how Jesus and his disciples handled a storm.**

Tell the story of Jesus stilling the storm, found in Mark 4:35-41.

Form groups of no more than five. Form only as many groups as you have jars. Say: **Let's try to make our own storm in these jars I've brought.**

Give each group a jar. Have children share the following duties. If you have fewer than five children in each group, some children may perform more than one duty.

Have one child in each group remove the lid from the jar. Have another child pour water into the jar until the jar is about two-thirds full. Have another child put a teaspoon of salt into the water. Have another child add one drop of dishwashing liquid to the salt water mixture. Have another child put the lid back on the jar. Show the children how to shake the liquid by holding the jar in both hands and moving the jar in a circle, using a stirring motion. The mixture should form a funnel. Have the children in each group take turns shaking the jar to create a storm.

Ask:

● **Tell about a time when you were afraid in a storm.** (I was afraid a tornado would pick up my house; I was afraid lightning would strike through my window.)

● **What makes people afraid?** (Things they don't understand; scary things; when they don't trust God; when they think they're going to get hurt.)

● **When are you afraid?** (When I go to bed, and it's dark in my room; when I'm in the house alone; when I have to walk through an alley.)

● **What can we do to calm our fears?** (Trust God; read the Bible; pray; talk with friends and family; think about good things.)

Say: **The disciples called to Jesus when they were afraid. He heard them and calmed the storm. When we are afraid, we can talk to Jesus, too. Jesus can calm our fears.**

Vanilla-Wafer Sandwiches

- -

STORY

Jesus feeds the 5,000 (John 6:1-15)

Jesus fed a hungry crowd of more than 5,000 people with the five loaves and two fish that a young boy shared. Children will learn that God can do wonderful things when we're willing to share.

THE EXPERIENCE

Ask:

● **When do you get really hungry?** (At lunch time; in the afternoon after school; after soccer practice.)

● **What do you do when you get hungry?** (Fix a snack; ask when dinner will be ready.)

Say: **We're going to hear a story now about a lot of hungry people.** Tell the story of Jesus feeding the 5,000, found in John 6:1-15.

<table>
<tr><td>

PREPARATION

You'll need:

● vanilla wafers,

● peanut butter,

● plastic knives,

● and paper towels.

</td></tr>
</table>

Ask:

● **What do you think the boy thought when he handed his food to Jesus?** (Jesus would give it back; Jesus would eat it.)

● **What do you think the boy thought when he saw all the people eating loaves and fish from what he shared?** (Amazed; happy; thankful.)

Say: **We're going to share some food now.**

Have children wash their hands. Give children each four vanilla wafers and a plastic knife. Help them spread peanut butter on two of their four wafers, then put one plain wafer on top of each of their peanut butter wafers. Tell children to keep one cookie sandwich and give one to a friend. If any children end up with more than two cookies, they must give their extra cookies away to children who only have one.

Ask:

● **How do you feel about sharing?** (I like to share, but it's hard to share my favorite things; I don't like to share my things with my brother because he might break them.)

● **Why is it important to share?** (So everyone can have what they need; so you won't have too much while someone else has nothing; because Jesus would share.)

● **What can you share?** (Toys; food; clothes; my house; friends.)

Say: **Because one little boy shared his loaves and fish with Jesus, many people were able to eat. God can use us to help many people when we share what we have. Let's remember to share this week.**

Walking Across

PREPARATION

You'll need:

● **an 8- to 10-foot-long 2×4**

● **and blindfolds.**

● **Before class, lay the board on the floor in the center of the room.**

STORY

Jesus walks on water (Matthew 14:22-33)

Jesus invited Peter to walk out on the water to meet him. But when Peter looked at the waves, he began to sink. As Peter sank, Jesus lifted him out. Children will learn from Peter's example that it's important to focus on Jesus instead of focusing on problems.

THE EXPERIENCE

As children arrive, let them try walking across the board (as if walking a tightrope). When you're ready to start, call the children together. Ask:

● **What was it like to walk on the board?** (It was hard because it's so narrow; it was fun to try and balance; it was easy once I got the hang of it.)

Form trios and have children line up at one end of the board. Blindfold one member of each trio. If you don't have enough blindfolds, have children take turns wearing them. Say: **If you're wearing a blindfold, your job is to walk across the board. The other two people in your trio will help you get up. If you step off the board, you have to go to the end of the line and wait your turn to start again.**

Let all children have one try. Most will step off the board after a few steps. Say: **Now I want you to walk across the board again. This time, your friends will stand on both sides of you to help.**

Position the other two members of the trio. Have them help the blindfolded child step onto the board and place his or her arms on their shoulders. Instruct them to help the child step back onto the board if he or she steps off.

When all children have walked across the board, ask:

● **What was it like to walk across the board blindfolded?** (Scary; I didn't know where I was going; embarrassing when I stepped off.)

● **Did it help to have your friends standing around you? Why or why not?** (Yes, my friends kept me from falling off; no, I still couldn't see.)

Say: **Even though you still couldn't see, it was a lot easier to walk across the board knowing you could trust your friends to help. Our story today is about a man who tried to walk across the water without help. Listen to hear what happened to him.**

Tell the story of Jesus and Peter walking on the water, found in Matthew 14:22-33.

Ask:

● **What do you think Peter was thinking as he walked on the water to Jesus?** (Look at me; this is scary; is this really happening?)

● **Why did Peter start to sink?** (The waves made him worry; he wasn't looking at Jesus; he wasn't trusting Jesus.)

● **What happens when you forget to trust Jesus?** (I get worried; I get depressed; I feel sorry for myself.)

● **Do you think your problems are important to Jesus? Why?** (Jesus cares about us; Jesus loves us; Jesus wants to help us.)

● **What should we do when we have problems?** (Pray; trust Jesus.)

Say: **As long as Peter remembered to trust Jesus, he could walk right through the waves. But when Peter looked around at the waves, he got scared and forgot to trust Jesus. If we focus only on our problems, sometimes we forget to trust Jesus. But if we remember to trust Jesus with our problems, he'll help us.**

Hands Wreath

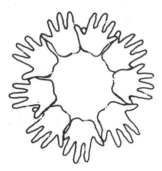

STORY

The good Samaritan (Luke 10:25-37)

Jesus showed that a Samaritan who helped a stranger was a better neighbor than the priest and the Levite who didn't help. Use this story to encourage children to follow the Samaritan's example by loving and serving others.

THE EXPERIENCE

Ask:

● **Do you know your neighbors? What are your neighbors like?**

Say: **A man once asked Jesus a question about his neighbors. Jesus answered the man by telling him this story.**

Tell the story of the good Samaritan, found in Luke 10:25-37. Explain to the children that most Samaritans wouldn't have helped the hurt man because Samaritans and Jews were enemies.

Ask:

● **Why do you think the Samaritan helped the hurt man?** (Because he felt sorry for him; maybe the man would help him someday when he needed it.)

Say: **We're going to make a special wreath for our door that will remind us of this story.**

Give children each a piece of construction paper, some crayons or markers, and scissors. Have children trace around both of their hands on the paper, cut the hand tracings out, and write their names on their hand cutouts. Then help children arrange the hands in a circle like a wreath, overlapping each cutout. Glue the hand cutouts in place. Tape the wreath to the door of your classroom.

Say: **We made our wreath out of hand prints because when we help or serve someone, we often use our hands.**

Ask:

● **How can we use our hands to help and serve?** (Cook something for someone; clean; draw a get-well card for someone who's sick.)

● **How can we use our voices to help and serve?** (Encourage someone; sing for people; be polite.)

Say: **The Samaritan saw someone who needed help, and he stopped to help. He was a true neighbor. We can be true neighbors by helping someone who needs our help. Let's look for people who need our help this week and be true neighbors to them by helping and serving them.**

I Can Help

STORY

Mary and Martha (Luke 10:38-42)

When Jesus visited Mary and Martha, Mary left her work to listen to Jesus. Children can listen to Jesus today by praying and reading the Bible. Use this story to help children make listening to Jesus an important priority in their lives.

THE EXPERIENCE

Ask:
- **Who does the chores or jobs at your house?**
- **What chores do you do at home?**

Say: **We're going to make charts to help us keep track of our jobs at home, and then we'll hear a story about someone who was worried about getting all the jobs done at her house.**

Distribute photocopies of the "I Can Help" handout. Have children fill in the blank lines with additional responsibilities they have at home, then cut out the chart from the bottom half of the handout. Combine equal parts unflavored gelatin and boiling water in the baking dish and show children how to paint the gelatin mixture onto the back of the top half of the handout.

Say: **After the glue dries, you can cut these out and use them as stickers to mark your progress with your jobs at home. Each time you do a job at home, write the day you did it and put a sticker in under that space on your chart. When you run out of stickers, you can use other stickers you have at home. While the glue is drying on our stickers, let's hear our story.**

Tell the story of Mary and Martha, found in Luke 10:38-42.

Ask:
- **How do you feel when you have a big job to do and no one helps you?** (Angry; frustrated; like I'll never get it finished.)
- **Why is it important to listen to Jesus?** (So we know what he wants us to do; to learn from him.)
- **Mary was able to sit right at Jesus' feet. How can we listen to Jesus today?** (By praying; by reading the Bible.)

Say: **Getting our jobs done at home is important, but listening to Jesus is even more important. Jesus said listening to him was the most important thing Mary could do. We can listen to Jesus today by praying and reading God's Word. Plan a time each day to listen to Jesus.**

GOOD JOB!	*JOB WELL DONE*	THANKS FOR HELPING	Good Worker!
GOOD JOB!	*JOB WELL DONE*	THANKS FOR HELPING	Good Worker!

I CAN HELP!

PICK UP MY ROOM.			
SET THE TABLE.			
HELP WITH THE DISHES.			

Popcorn Cones

STORY

A rich man builds bigger barns (Luke 12:13-21)

A rich man built bigger barns to store his great harvest so he could have an easy life. But before he could enjoy everything he'd stored away, he died. Use this story to teach children to share what they have with others.

THE EXPERIENCE

● **What do farmers grow on their farms?** (Vegetables; wheat; corn.)

Say: **Our story today is about a farmer who grew grain. Corn is one kind of grain that's good to eat. I've brought some popcorn for a snack today. Let's make cones to hold our popcorn.**

Give children each a semicircle and show them how to roll it into a cone. While the children are stapling their cones, roll the large semicircle into a cone for yourself. Make sure children see that your cone is bigger. Put a few kernels of popped popcorn in each child's cone, then fill the large cone you've made for yourself. Set your cone where children can see it during the story, but don't eat any of the popcorn. Place any extra popcorn out of sight.

As children are eating their popcorn, tell the story of the rich man's barns, found in Luke 12:13-21.

Say: **In a minute we're going to talk about this story. But first, would anyone like more popcorn?**

Look around for the extra popcorn for a moment, then say: **I guess we're all out of popcorn. Sorry about that.**

Sit down in front of the children and start eating popcorn from your large cone.

Ask:

● **What can we learn from this story?** (Not to be greedy; to share what we have.)

● **Do you think that means I should share my popcorn?**

Divide your popcorn among the children, then ask:

● **The rich man in this story had plenty of grain. What do we have plenty of?** (Food; toys; clothes; popcorn.)

● **How can we share what we have with others?** (Give away stuff we can't use; invite people to come to our houses.)

Say: **God gave the rich man a great harvest so he could share with others, not so he could keep it all himself. We can share what we have with others, too.**

PREPARATION

You'll need:

● popped popcorn,
● construction paper,
● one large sheet of construction paper,
● and a stapler.
● Before class, cut the construction paper into semicircles. Use the large sheet of construction paper to cut one large semicircle.

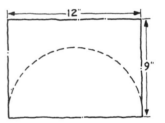

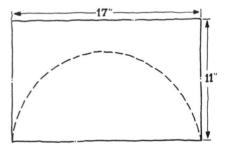

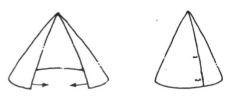

Find a Coin

PREPARATION

You'll need:

- various coins
- and a bag of candy coins.
- Children will especially enjoy seeing foreign coins, if you can find them. Before class, hide the coins around the room. Place the candy coins out of sight but within easy reach.

STORY

The lost coin (Luke 15:8-10)

A woman lost a coin and searched until she found it. Then she called her friends to rejoice with her. Jesus said the angels in heaven rejoice when a sinner changes his or her heart. Use this story to teach children to be happy for others who change their hearts and decide to follow God.

THE EXPERIENCE

Ask:

- **Tell about a time when you lost something.**
- **Where are good places to look for things you've lost?** (In couches or big chairs; under furniture; in closets.)

Say: **I've lost some coins in our room today. Can you help me find them?**

Give children several minutes to find the coins. After children have found the coins, invite them to show the coins they've found as you collect them. Then say: **Thank you so much for helping me find my coins! Let's have a party to celebrate!**

Take out the bag of candy coins and shower them over the children. Make sure the coins are distributed fairly, then say: **Our story today is about a woman who looked for a lost coin, like we just did.**

Tell the story of the woman who lost her coin, found in Luke 15:8-10.

Ask:

- **Why do you think the woman spent so much time looking for one coin when she had nine others?** (Maybe she needed to buy something that cost 10 coins; she knew it had to be somewhere in the house.)
- **How is the woman's looking for one lost coin like God's looking for people to follow him?** (God never stops looking for us; God wants everybody to find him and follow him.)
- **How is the way the woman felt when she found her coin like the way God might feel when people decide to follow him?** (God is happy when people decide to follow him; maybe God tells everybody in heaven.)
- **What are some ways we can celebrate and be happy for people when they decide to follow God?** (Have a party; give them a hug; remind them of God's promises.)

Say: **God rejoices when people change their hearts and decide to follow him. We can rejoice, too, and help others celebrate when they decide to follow God.**

Heart Stencil

STORY

The lost son (Luke 15:11-32)

A boy left home to spend his inheritance as he pleased. But later he saw that he was better off at home. When he returned, his forgiving father welcomed him home. The forgiving father in this story will help children see that they can ask God's forgiveness when they've done something wrong.

THE EXPERIENCE

Ask: **How do you feel when someone tells you what to do?** (Mad; I want to do things my way; I usually do it.)

Say: **We're going to hear a story today about a boy who left home so no one could tell him what to do.**

Tell the story of the lost son, found in Luke 15:11-32.

● **When the son finally decided to go back home, what did he think would happen?** (He thought he wouldn't be welcome; he thought he'd have to be a servant.)

● **How did the father treat his son when he came home?** (He hugged him; he gave him a robe and a ring; he had a party for him.)

● **Do you think the son deserved to be treated so nicely? Why or why not?** (No, because he wasted all his dad's money; yes, his dad still loved him.)

● **How do you think the son felt when his father forgave him?** (Surprised; grateful; happy.)

● **How do you feel when someone forgives you?** (Good; relieved; thankful.)

Say: **God is like the father in our story. If we ask, he's always willing to forgive us. We're going to make heart stencils to help us remember God's forgiveness.**

Cover the tables with newspaper. Give children each two sheets of construction paper. Have children each draw a heart on one sheet of construction paper, cut it out, and tape it to their other sheet of construction paper. Make sure the tape is completely covered by the heart. Distribute paint and paintbrushes and have children paint over the heart and the paper around it.

Say: **Think of the bad things we do as being the paint you put on the clean heart you taped to the page. What happens to your heart when you do bad things?** (It gets dirty; it gets mean.)

Help children carefully pull their painted hearts off the paper to reveal a clean, unpainted heart underneath. Say: **The clean heart underneath is like God's forgiveness. When we ask God to forgive us, he'll make our hearts clean and pure again.**

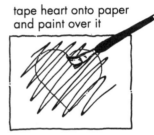

tape heart onto paper and paint over it

lift heart off to reveal clean heart underneath

Thank You Envelopes

PREPARATION

You'll need:

- photocopies of the envelope pattern (p. 85),
- scissors,
- tape,
- and crayons or markers.
- You may want to practice folding an envelope before class.

STORY

The 10 sick men (Luke 17:11-19)

Ten sick men cried out to Jesus, asking him to heal them. But after they'd been healed, only one man came back to thank Jesus. Use this story to encourage children to thank God for the good things he's done for them.

THE EXPERIENCE

Say:

● **Tell about a thank you note you've written or a time you remembered to thank someone. Today we're going to hear a story about someone who delivered his "thank you" in person.**

Tell the story of the 10 sick men, found in Luke 17:11-19.

Ask:

● **How do you feel when you've done something nice for someone and they don't remember to thank you?** (Sad; forgotten; like they don't really care.)

● **How do you think Jesus felt?**

● **Why do you think nine men didn't thank Jesus?** (They were so excited they forgot; they couldn't believe they were really healed.)

Say: **The man who came back to thank Jesus was grateful for the wonderful thing Jesus had done for him. Think of someone who has done something nice for you. We're going to make thank you cards to send to those people now.**

Distribute photocopies of the envelope pattern. Have children cut out the envelope pattern, write their thank you messages and decorate the envelopes with crayons or markers. Make sure they leave room to write an address on the front panel. Demonstrate how to fold the envelope and seal it with tape. As children work, ask:

● **What are you thankful for?** (My family; my pet; school holidays.)

● **What are some ways we can tell God we're thankful?** (Pray; tell God thank you; don't complain.)

When children have finished their notes, set them aside and form a circle. Say: **Let's thank God for the special people in our lives. We'll each pray, "God, thank you for _____ ." When it's your turn, fill in the name of the person you wrote your thank you note to.**

When all children have shared, close by saying "Amen." Encourage children to deliver their thank you notes this week.

Thank You!

_____

_____

_____

_____

_____

Prayer Booklet

PREPARATION

You'll need:

- ● **construction paper,**
- ● **typing paper,**
- ● **pencils,**
- ● **crayons,**
- ● **scissors,**
- ● **a hole punch,**
- ● **and yarn.**

cut typing paper and construction paper this way

cut on dotted line

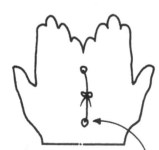

- ● stack cutouts
- ● punch 2 holes
- ● thread yarn through and tie

close to make booklet

STORY

The Pharisee and the tax collector pray (Luke 18:9-14)

A Pharisee thanked God he was better than other men, but a tax collector asked God for mercy because he had sinned. Jesus said the tax collector's humble prayer pleased God. Children will learn to focus their prayers on God rather than on themselves.

THE EXPERIENCE

Ask:

- ● **What is prayer?** (Talking to God; asking for God's help; thanking God.)
- ● **What do you hear people pray about most often?** (They ask God to help someone who's sick; they ask God to help them with things.)

Say: **We're going to make a prayer booklet you can use to write down or draw things you want to pray about.**

Give children each a pencil, scissors, one sheet of construction paper, and two sheets of typing paper. Have children fold their typing paper in half. Have them each place one hand on the paper, little finger on the fold. Then have them each trace around their hand and cut it out, being careful not to cut on the fold.

Using the hand cutout as a pattern, help children fold and cut their other papers the same way. Have children tuck the typing paper cutouts inside the construction paper cutouts to make a booklet. Punch two holes in each child's booklet along the fold. Help children thread yarn through the holes and tie it.

Say: **Now we're going to hear a story about two people who prayed very different prayers.**

Tell the story of the Pharisee and the tax collector, found in Luke 18:9-14. Explain that people looked up to the Pharisees because they were the religious leaders of the community. People hated tax collectors because they often collected extra money for themselves.

After you've finished telling the story, say:

- ● **Show me what you would look like if you said, "Thank you, God, that I'm so great!"**
- ● **Show me what you would look like if you said, "God, I know I've done wrong things. Please forgive me."**

Ask:

- ● **Which prayer pleased God? Explain.** (The tax collector's prayer, because he admitted he'd done wrong things; he asked God to forgive him.)
- ● **What was wrong with the Pharisee's prayer?** (He was bragging when he should have been asking God for help; he was saying bad

things about other people.)

Say: **Think of something you want to pray about. Then write a prayer in your booklet that you think would please God.**

Be sure to help younger children who haven't learned to write yet. Give children time to write their prayers, then say: **God wants our prayers to focus on him, not on ourselves. When you pray this week, remember the tax collector and focus on God.**

Getting to the Treasure

----- ----- ----- ----- ----- ----- ----- ----- -----

STORY

Jesus and the children (Mark 10:13-16)

Jesus' disciples told children not to bother him. But Jesus told the children to come. He held them and blessed them. Use this story to teach children that they can come to Jesus any time.

THE EXPERIENCE

Say: **Today we're going to take a short trip to get a special treat.**

Place the treat box on one side of the room. Have the children line up on the other side of the room. Help them make a barrier of tables, chairs, and pillows in the center of the room between themselves and the treat box.

Say: **Our special treat is on the other side of this barrier. To get our treat, we'll each have to get across. You can each cross the barrier in your own way. For example, you might want to climb over the chairs or crawl under the table. Only one person may cross at a time. After we've all crossed, we'll have our treat.**

When all children have crossed the barrier, ask:

● **How would you feel if I said we don't have time for a treat?** (Disappointed; frustrated; mad.)

● **How would you feel if I said this treat is only for adults?** (Angry; sad; disappointed.)

Say: **That's the way the children in our Bible story felt.**

Pass out the treats. As the children are eating, tell the story of Jesus and the children, found in Mark 10:13-16.

Ask:

● **How does Jesus feel about children?** (Jesus loves children; Jesus wants children to be his friends.)

● **How do you think the children felt when they couldn't get to Jesus?** (Sad; angry; left out.)

● **How was crossing the barrier to get to the treats like the children trying to get to Jesus?** (The children had to get around all the people; the children were excited to see Jesus, and we were excited to get a treat.)

● **If Jesus were sitting in our classroom right now, what do you think he'd do?** (Hug us; laugh and play with us; teach us.)

Say: **Jesus wanted to be with the children. He held them and blessed them. Jesus wants to be with you, too. You're very important to him. He wants you to talk with him any time you want. When no one else will listen, Jesus will. When no one else cares, Jesus cares. He will never stop loving you.**

Blind Tag

PREPARATION

You'll need:

● a blindfold for each child.

STORY

Jesus heals a blind man (Mark 10:46-52)

Bartimaeus heard that Jesus was passing by, so he called to Jesus for mercy. People told Bartimaeus to be quiet, but he kept calling until Jesus stopped and healed him. Use this story to encourage children to be persistent in their prayers.

THE EXPERIENCE

Blindfold children as they arrive. When all children have arrived, say: **Our story today is about a man who couldn't see. We're going to wear blindfolds during our class today to see what that was like.**

Form pairs. Have children identify themselves to their partners, then spread the children out around the room. Say: **We're going to play a game. Your job is to find your partner by calling his or her name. When you hear your name, call out your partner's name. Keep walking in the direction of your partner's voice until you find each other. Ready? Go.**

Watch the children carefully to make sure they don't trip or run into anything. Steer children in the right direction if they're having a hard time. When all children have found their partners, have them sit down where they are but don't remove their blindfolds.

Ask:

● **Was it easy or hard to find your partner? Why?** (Easy, because she was standing right next to me; hard, because I wasn't sure where his voice was coming from.)

● **How did you finally find your partner?** (I just kept calling my partner's name; we ran into each other; you pointed us in the right direction.)

Say: **We're going to hear a story now about a blind man who kept calling until he found Jesus.**

Tell the story of Bartimaeus, found in Mark 10:46-52. When you tell about Jesus' restoration of Bartimaeus' sight, remove the children's blindfolds.

Ask:

● **How did you feel when I removed your blindfold?** (Good; glad to be able to see again; surprised at how bright the light was.)

● **How do you think Bartimaeus felt when Jesus healed him?** (Excited to see all the things around him; thankful; surprised; happy.)

● **Why did Bartimaeus keep calling Jesus?** (He knew Jesus could heal him; he didn't know where Jesus was since he couldn't see.)

● **How can we call Jesus today?** (By praying; by singing songs to Jesus.)

Say: **Bartimaeus kept calling until Jesus answered him. When we call to God in prayer, God will answer us, too. The Bible promises that God will meet all our needs.**

Cone Trees

STORY

Zacchaeus (Luke 19:1-10)

Zacchaeus wanted to see Jesus passing through his town. But because he was a small man and couldn't see over the heads of the crowd, he watched from a tree. Jesus stopped at the tree and told Zacchaeus he wanted to stay at his house that day. When children hear how Jesus accepted a man no one else cared about, they'll be encouraged to accept others.

THE EXPERIENCE

Ask:

● **How many different kinds of trees can you think of?** (Pine trees; apple trees; palm trees.)

● **Tell about what it's like to climb a tree.**

Say: **We're going to make trees that we can eat, and then we'll hear a story about a man who climbed a tree.**

Give children each a square of waxed paper to use as a place mat, a paper cup, and a plastic knife. Help children put a spoonful of frosting in their cups, add a drop of green food coloring, and stir. Distribute sugar cones and show children how to turn their cones upside down and spread frosting on them.

Let children enjoy their cone trees as you tell the story of Zacchaeus, found in Luke 19:1-10.

Ask:

● **What would you do if you weren't tall enough to see in a crowd?** (Stand on someone else's shoulders; try to get to the front;

PREPARATION

You'll need:

● pointed, sugar ice cream cones;

● plastic knives;

● waxed paper;

● paper towels;

● small paper cups;

● a spoon;

● green food coloring;

● and canned frosting.

● You can use canned frosting, or you can make frosting by mixing ½ pound of powdered sugar, 2 egg whites, and ¼ teaspoon cream of tartar. Blend the ingredients together, then beat for 7 to 10 minutes at high speed. Store in the refrigerator in a tightly covered container. This frosting dries and hardens quickly.

sugar cone,
upside down

paint with frosting

climb a tree like Zacchaeus.)

● **Why didn't the people like Zacchaeus?** (Because he took their money; they were jealous because he had an important job.)

● **How do you think Zacchaeus felt when Jesus spoke to him?** (Excited; amazed; happy.)

● **What did Jesus think of Zacchaeus?** (Jesus loved him; Jesus wanted to help him.)

Say: **Nobody cared about Zacchaeus. But Jesus did. Jesus accepted Zacchaeus. We can follow Jesus' example and love and accept people around us.**

Bread-Stick Faces

PREPARATION

You'll need:

● **two sticks of refrigerated ready-made bread-stick dough for each child,**

● **aluminum foil,**

● **paper towels,**

● **a cookie sheet,**

● **a potholder,**

● **and an oven.**

STORY

Jesus raises Lazarus (John 11:1-44)

When Jesus went to Lazarus' tomb, he cried. Then Jesus called to his friend Lazarus, and Lazarus came back to life. Children will learn from this story that Jesus understands our feelings.

THE EXPERIENCE

Say: **Show me what kind of face you'd make if I said:**
● **Let's go out for ice cream.**
● **Take out a pencil and paper. We're going to have a test.**
● **You have the measles.**
● **Grandma and Grandpa are coming to visit.**
● **I have a special present for you.**
Ask:
● **Do you think Jesus had the same kinds of feelings we do? Explain.**

Say: **We're going to make bread-stick faces to show how we're feeling, and then we'll hear a sad story with a happy ending.**

Have children wash their hands. Preheat the oven to the temperature indicated on the bread dough package.

Give children each a small square of aluminum foil and two sticks of bread dough. Show them how to pinch off two small pieces for eyes and one larger piece for a mouth. Then help them roll the remaining dough into a long snake and then form it into a circle. Have children each shape their eyes and mouth to show a feeling such as happiness, sadness, or anger and place them inside their circle to make a face.

Have children place their foil squares on the cookie sheet and bake the bread-stick faces according to the package instructions. If you don't have an oven in your room, ask a teacher or a helper to take the bread-stick faces to the oven and return them when they are done.

While the bread-stick faces are baking, tell the story of Jesus raising Lazarus, found in John 11:1-44.

Ask:

● **Why do you think Jesus cried?** (He was sorry for Lazarus; he was sorry for Mary and Martha; he missed Lazarus.)

● **Do you think Jesus ever laughed? Why or why not?**

● **Do you think Jesus knows how you feel? Why or why not?** (Yes, because Jesus knows everything; no, I have different feelings than people who lived a long time ago.)

Give children paper towels and distribute the bread-stick faces. Say: **Jesus cried when his friend Lazarus died. When Jesus lived on earth he had feelings, just as we do. So when you look at the expression on your bread-stick face, remember that Jesus knows and understands that feeling.**

on foil

Clothespin Donkey

STORY

Jesus enters Jerusalem on a colt (Matthew 21:1-11)

As Jesus rode into Jerusalem, people spread branches and cloaks on the road, treating him like a king. They shouted praises to Jesus. Use this story to encourage children to praise and worship Jesus.

THE EXPERIENCE

Ask:

● **What animals can people ride?** (Horses; big dogs; bulls in rodeos; elephants in zoos.)

● **Tell about a time when you rode on an animal.**

Say: **In Bible times, people often rode on donkeys. We're going to make a clothespin donkey, and then we'll hear a story about a time when Jesus rode on a donkey.**

Set out glue. Give children each three clothespins and help them glue the clothespins together to make a donkey. Give children each a brown bead or button to glue on for a nose and yarn to glue on for a tail. Then have children draw eyes and color in the middle of the ears. If you're using craft eyes, help children glue these on.

Tell the story of Jesus riding into Jerusalem on a colt, found in Matthew 21:1-11.

Ask:

● **Why did the people shout and lay their coats in the road when they saw Jesus coming?** (They wanted to show respect for Jesus; they were excited to see Jesus; they were too hot.)

● **What is praise?** (Telling Jesus how great he is; letting Jesus know we love him.)

PREPARATION

For each child, you'll need:

● **three wooden craft clothespins,**

● **two inches of brown yarn,**

● **a small brown bead or button,**

● **a brown or black marker,**

● **and glue.**

● **You may also choose to provide two craft eyes for each child.**

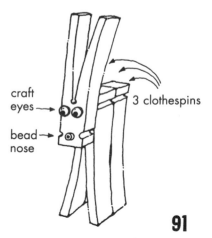

craft eyes →

bead → nose

3 clothespins

● **Why do we praise and worship Jesus?** (Because of the great things he's done; because he's God's son; because he died for us.)

Say: **The people who saw Jesus coming treated him like a king. They were hoping he would become king of their country, so they honored him and praised him. Jesus is king. But he is king over more than just a country. Jesus is the king of all kings, the ruler of all the universe. And Jesus is a good king—strong and loving. Let's remember to praise and worship Jesus this week!**

Encourage children to use their donkeys as Easter decorations, or put them in their Easter baskets.

Cinnamon Cookies

PREPARATION

You'll need:

● refrigerated sugar-cookie dough,

● ½ teaspoon cinnamon,

● ¼ cup sugar,

● a knife,

● a spoon,

● a pie plate,

● paper towels,

● waxed paper,

● a cookie sheet,

● an oven,

● a potholder,

● plastic sandwich bags,

● gift-wrap ribbon,

● and scissors.

● Before class, mix the cinnamon and sugar in the pie pan.

STORY

The widow's offering (Mark 12:41-44)

A poor widow put only two small coins into the temple offering box. But Jesus said she gave more than all the others, because she gave all the money she had. Use this story to encourage children to give what they have cheerfully.

THE EXPERIENCE

Ask:

● **Raise your hand if you get an allowance. What do you have to do to get your allowance?** (Clean my room; do my chores; nothing.)

● **How do you spend the money you get?** (I buy comic books; I buy candy; I save it to spend on vacation.)

Say: **We're going to hear a story now about a woman who gave away all the money she had.**

Tell the story of the widow's coins, found in Mark 12:41-44.

Ask:

● **Do you think it was easy for the woman to give away that money? Why or why not?** (No, because it was all she had; yes, she just dropped it in the box.)

● **Why do people give money at church?** (For missionaries; to pay the minister; because God wants us to.)

● **What else can we give besides money?** (Food; clothes; help.)

Say: **We're going to make cinnamon cookies to give away. While we make them, think of someone you'd like to give your cookies to.**

Have children wash their hands. Preheat the oven according to directions on the package of dough. Give children each a square of waxed paper to work on and a slice of cookie dough. Show children how to roll their dough into a ball, roll it in the cinnamon and sugar mixture, and put it on the cookie sheet. Let children make as many cookies as possible.

Bake the cookies according to the package instructions. If you don't have an oven in your room, ask a helper to take the cookies to the oven and bring them back when they're done.

Divide the cookies equally among the children. Let children each eat one cookie, then help them put their remaining cookies in sandwich bags and tie the tops with ribbon.

Ask:
- **Who did you decide to give your cookies to?**
- **How do you feel when someone gives you something special?** (Thankful; happy; like I want to give something, too.)
- **How do you feel when you give someone else something?** (Good; it's fun; like I'm making a surprise.)
- **Why does God want us to give?** (To help others; to share what we have.)

Say: **The woman in our story gave all the money she had. The Bible says God is pleased when we give cheerfully. Be sure to give a big smile when you give your cookies.**

Soap and Water

STORY

Jesus washes the disciples' feet (John 13:1-17)

When Jesus wanted to teach his disciples how to be servants, he wrapped a towel around his waist and washed their feet. Children will learn that they can serve other people just as Jesus served his disciples.

THE EXPERIENCE

Ask:
- **What would you use to clean clothes?**
- **What would you use to clean dishes?**

Say: **We're going to do an experiment to see how soap acts in water, and then we'll hear a story about a special cleaning job.**

Give children each a plastic bowl half-filled with water and help them sprinkle pepper over the water's surface. Show them how to drip one drop of dishwashing liquid from a spoon into the center of their bowl. Watch what happens.

Say: **Water has a kind of "skin" at the top called "surface tension," where the molecules are pulled together tightly. The pepper sits on top of this surface. But when the dishwashing liquid drops in, it breaks the surface, and the pepper scoots away from the center to where there is more surface tension.**

Have children set their bowls aside and form a circle. Say: **Our story today is about a special cleaning job Jesus did.**

Tell the story of Jesus washing his disciples' feet from John 13:1-17.

PREPARATION

You'll need:
- plastic bowls and spoons,
- a pitcher of water,
- ground black pepper,
- dishwashing liquid,
- and paper towels.

Ask:

● **Why did Jesus wash his friends' feet?** (To help them; to show them how to act; to be kind.)

Say: **Jesus washed his friends' feet to teach them how to serve others. Just like the pepper moved away from the soap in our activity, Jesus' friends spread out to serve others and tell them about Jesus.**

Ask:

● **What does it mean to serve others?** (To help them; to think of others before yourself.)

● **How can you serve your family?** (Wash dishes; take out trash; do extra jobs around the house without being asked.)

● **How can you serve your friends?** (Help them with chores; let them have first choice of snacks; let them ride my bike.)

● **Why would we want to serve others?** (To be like Jesus; to help them; it makes me feel good to help.)

Say: **Jesus washed his friends' feet to show them that if he could serve them, they could serve others. Jesus wants us to serve others, too.**

Gather the children in a circle. Say: **Let's spread out to serve others this week. When I count to three, we'll put our hands together in the center of our circle and say "Serve!" One, two, three!**

Reminders

PREPARATION

You'll need:

● **a pillowcase into which you have placed**
● **a book,**
● **a stuffed toy,**
● **a birthday candle,**
● **a hat or cap,**
● **mittens,**
● **a valentine card,**
● **a map or road atlas,**
● **an empty medicine bottle,**
● **and a Christmas ornament.**

STORY

The Last Supper (Luke 22:7-20)

At Jesus' last dinner with his friends, he ate bread and drank wine with them. He told his friends to remember him whenever they ate bread and drank wine. Use this story to encourage children to remember Jesus.

THE EXPERIENCE

Say: **We're going to find out what we can remember today.**

Hold out the pillowcase and ask a child to come and reach into it and pull something out. Ask the child to tell you what that item reminds him or her of. Let each child have a turn.

Say: **Each of the things in this pillowcase reminded us of something special. Our story today is about some things Jesus gave us to remind us of him.**

Tell the story of the Last Supper found in Luke 22:7-20.

Ask:

● **What do you think Jesus wants us to remember about him?** (That he died for our sins; how he treated people; things he said.)

● **Why does Jesus want us to remember him?** (So we'll keep him first in our lives; so we can try to be like him.)

Say: **Jesus told his disciples to remember him when they ate the bread and drank the wine. He wants us to remember him, too. When we remember Jesus, we're not just remembering someone who lived long ago and died for us one day. We're remembering that Jesus is alive and loves us and cares about us. Jesus wants us to remember what he did for us and to remember he's here for us now.**

Tree of Life

STORY

The Crucifixion (Matthew 27:32-61; Romans 4:25; 5:8)

After he was betrayed by one of his own disciples, Jesus was tried and put to death on a cross. Jesus' death was a time of great sadness for his disciples. But his resurrection was a time of great joy. Children will learn that Jesus' resurrection is something they can be happy about, too.

THE EXPERIENCE

Ask:

● **Can you think of a time when you were really sad? Tell about it.** (When my cat got run over by a car; when my grandpa died; when my parents got a divorce.)

Say: **Our story today is about a time when Jesus' followers were very sad.**

Tell the story of the Crucifixion found in Matthew 24:32-61. Further explanation of the Crucifixion is found in Romans 4:25; 5:8. Be careful how you tell this story, as many of the events leading up to the crucifixion may be frightening to younger children. Details like Jesus carrying his own cross and the darkness that accompanied Jesus' death will enhance the story for children. Omit violent details, such as beatings, where possible.

Say: **We're going to make a picture to help us remember this story.**

Distribute construction paper and crayons or markers and have children draw a wide hill on the paper. Pour brown paint into the bottom of several pie pans and demonstrate how to dip a sponge strip into the paint, then press it onto the paper to make a vertical print on the hill. Stamp the sponge horizontally over the first print to make a cross. Have children make three crosses on the hill they've drawn.

Ask:

● **How do you feel when you see your crosses and remember that Jesus died?** (Sad; sorry; I wish Jesus didn't have to die.)

Say: **Jesus' followers were sad when he died. But a few days**

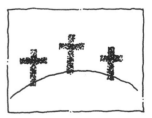

leaf pattern cut
from sponge strip

later they stopped being sad and started being happy. When some women went to visit Jesus' grave, they discovered that Jesus was alive again!

The wooden cross that Jesus died on was probably made from a dead tree. Let's add some leaves to one of our crosses to bring it back to life and remind us that Jesus didn't stay dead.

Pour green paint into the remaining pie pans. Cut the ends of the sponges into leaf shapes and help children stamp leaves on one of their crosses.

Ask:

● **How do you feel when you see your cross with the leaves and remember that Jesus is alive?** (Good; happy; excited.)

Say: **When Jesus left heaven to come to earth as a man, he knew he'd have to die one day. But he also knew he'd be alive again. Jesus' followers were very happy when they heard the news that he was alive. This good news can make us happy, too.**

Close in prayer, thanking God for the good news of Jesus' resurrection.

Paper Angels

PREPARATION

You'll need:

● **white typing paper,**

● **scissors,**

● **clear tape,**

● **white plastic spoons,**

● **permanent markers,**

● **yarn,**

● **and a stapler.**

● **Before class, cut a semicircle out of the typing paper for each child.**

roll paper into a cone

yarn hair

insert spoon handle into cone and draw face on bowl of spoon

STORY

The angel at the tomb (Matthew 27:62–28:10)

On the third day after Jesus' death, an angel came to the tomb and rolled the stone away. The tomb was empty. Jesus had risen. This lesson will help children understand that Jesus has power over death and that they can look forward to eternal life with him.

THE EXPERIENCE

Ask:

● **When the sun rises, what does the sky look like?**

Say: **Today we're going to hear about what happened at sunrise on one of the happiest days in history.**

Tell the story of Jesus' resurrection found in Matthew 27:62–28:10.

● **How do you think Mary felt when she heard the angel's news?** (Surprised; excited; she probably wondered how it happened.)

Say: **We're going to make paper angels to help us remember this story.**

Distribute the paper semicircles. Show children how to make a cone by rolling the paper and taping it in place. Insert the handle of a plastic spoon into the narrow end of the cone. Have children draw faces on their spoons with markers.

Set out several 2-inch lengths of yarn to tape to the bowl of the spoon to make hair. Demonstrate how to fold another sheet of paper accordion-style, staple it in the middle, and spread out the ends to make wings. Help children tape the wings to the back of their cones.

Ask:

● **Why is it important that Jesus rose from the dead?** (Because he's alive today; so we can be with him in heaven.)

Say: **Because Jesus died for us and rose again, we can live with him in heaven forever. Each time you see your angel, think of all the angels waiting with Jesus in heaven for you.**

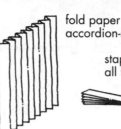
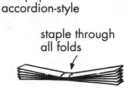
fold paper accordion-style

staple through all folds

tape to back of cone

Joy Biscuits

STORY

Peter and John heal a man who couldn't walk (Acts 3:1-10)

A man who couldn't walk asked Peter and John for money. They didn't have any money to give him, but they had something better. In Jesus' name, they told him to walk. Immediately, the man began to walk. Children will learn from this story to praise God for the things in their lives that give them joy.

THE EXPERIENCE

Ask:

● **Why do we need money?** (For food; so we can buy things.)

● **How do we get money?** (Working; allowance; saving.)

Say: **In Bible times, when people couldn't work to earn money because of blindness or a broken leg, they often had to beg. Listen to hear what happened when Peter and John met a man who was begging.**

Tell the story of Peter and John healing the man who couldn't walk, found in Acts 3:1-10.

Ask:

● **Why did the man jump and shout and praise God?** (Because he could walk again; because he knew God had healed him.)

Say: **The man in our story jumped for joy because he was healed. We're going to make joy biscuits to help us remember this story.**

Have children wash their hands. Preheat the oven to the temperature suggested on the package of dough. Lightly spray foil squares with cooking-oil spray and distribute them to the children to use as a work surface. Give children each dough for one biscuit. Have them take turns using the rolling pin to roll their biscuits flat. Set out raisins and help children write the word "joy" on their biscuits.

Put the biscuits on the cookie sheet and bake them until they're golden. If you don't have an oven in your room, ask a teacher or helper to take the biscuits to an oven and return them when they're done.

While the biscuits are baking, ask:

PREPARATION

You'll need:

● **refrigerated ready-made biscuit dough,**

● **one or more rolling pins,**

● **aluminum foil,**

● **cooking-oil spray,**

● **raisins,**

● **paper towels,**

● **an oven,**

● **a cookie sheet,**

● **and a potholder.**

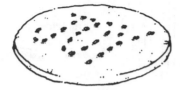

raisins on flattened biscuit dough

● **What is joy?** (Happiness; peace; gladness.)
● **What do you look like when you feel joyful?**
● **When do you feel joyful?** (When I'm with good friends; when I'm doing something I like; when I come to church.)

Say: **The man in our story felt joyful and praised God when he was able to walk again. When we think about all the good things God has done for us, we can rejoice and praise God, too.**

Play a joyful game with the children until the biscuits are done. As you distribute the biscuits, have each child share one thing that makes him or her feel joyful. Close in prayer, thanking God for all the good things he's done for the children.

Chariot Wheels

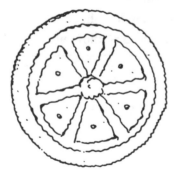

cheese spread squirted onto round crackers

STORY

Philip and the Ethiopian (Acts 8:26-40)

Philip met an Ethiopian man traveling in a chariot, reading scripture. Philip told him about Jesus, and the man became a Christian. When they hear how Philip told the Ethiopian about Jesus, children will be encouraged to tell others about Jesus, too.

THE EXPERIENCE

Ask:
● **What kind of transportation could you use to travel across the country?** (Car; bus; train; airplane.)
● **If you lived in Bible times and wanted to travel, what kinds of transportation could you choose from?** (Walking; riding a horse; a chariot.)

Say: **A few people in Bible times drove chariots. Today we're going to make chariot wheels we can eat. Then we'll hear a story about a man who rode in a chariot.**

Have children wash their hands. Form as many groups as you have cans of cheese spread. Distribute paper towels and crackers. Show children how to squirt the cheese on the crackers to look like spokes on a wheel. Have them take turns using the cans of cheese spread.

Let the children eat their crackers while you tell the story of Philip and the Ethiopian, found in Acts 8:26-40.

Ask:
● **What do you think Philip told the Ethiopian?** (About God sending Jesus; about Jesus' death; about how wonderful Jesus was.)
● **What would you tell someone who wanted to know about Jesus?** (That Jesus loves them; that Jesus can be their friend.)

Say: **Philip told the Ethiopian about Jesus, and he decided to be a Christian. We can tell other people about Jesus, too. Think** of someone you can tell about Jesus this week.

Close in prayer, asking God to help the children tell their friends about Jesus.

Silhouettes

STORY

Paul on the road to Damascus (Acts 9:1-19)

As Paul was on the way to Damascus to arrest Jesus' followers, Jesus spoke to him, and he became a Christian. Children will learn from this story that Jesus can change their hearts just as he changed Paul's heart.

THE EXPERIENCE

Ask:
● **How are you like other people in your family?**
● **How are you different from other people in your family?**
● **If you could change one thing about yourself, what would you change?** (I'd make myself older so my sister wouldn't boss me around; I'd like to have straight hair instead of curly hair; I'd get rid of my freckles.)

Say: **We can't change the way we look, but we can change the way we think or act. Our story today is about a man who changed the way he acted.**

Tell the story of Paul on the road to Damascus, found in Acts 9:1-20.

Ask:
● **How did Paul decide to change?** (He saw a bright light; Jesus told him to.)
● **What was different about Paul after he met Jesus on the road?** (He believed in Jesus; he stopped trying to kill Jesus' followers; he started preaching about Jesus.)

Say: **Before Paul met Jesus, his heart was full of hate, but Jesus was able to change Paul's heart. Meeting Jesus changed Paul's life. We're going to make heart-pocket silhouettes to remind us that Jesus can change our hearts and lives, too.**

Distribute crayons or markers, scissors, and photocopies of the "Heart Pockets" handout. Say: **Color and cut out the small hearts that show ways you'd like Jesus to change your heart. You might want to ask Jesus to put love or joy in your heart, for example. Then cut out the large heart pocket. As you're working I'll be drawing your silhouettes one at a time. After I've drawn your silhouette, cut it out and glue it to a sheet of construction paper. Then staple your heart pocket to the silhouette and tuck the small hearts you've chosen into the pocket.**

As children are working on their hearts, have one child at a time come

PREPARATION

You'll need:

● photocopies of the "Heart Pockets" handout (p. 100),
● crayons or markers,
● various colors of construction paper,
● black construction paper,
● scissors,
● tape,
● glue,
● an overhead projector or other source of strong light,
● and a pencil or marker.

Heart Pockets

to you so you can draw his or her silhouette. To draw the silhouettes, tape a sheet of black construction paper to a wall or bulletin board and aim the projector light toward it. Have the child stand sideways in front of the paper so his or her shadow is cast onto the paper. Draw around the shadow and give the paper to the child to cut out.

After all children have completed their silhouettes and heart pockets, say: **Paul had done many wrong things, but Jesus completely changed him. If we've done wrong, Jesus can change us, too. But we have to be willing to change. Let's ask Jesus to change our hearts and help us do right.**

Close by having children complete the following sentence prayer by reading from one of the hearts in their heart pocket: Dear God, Please put _____ in my heart this week. Amen.

Ball Toss

STORY

Paul escapes in a basket (Acts 9:23-25)

When some Jews plotted to kill Paul, his friends helped him escape by lowering him over the city wall in a basket. This story will encourage children to look for ways to help their friends.

PREPARATION

You'll need:
● a large bedsheet
● and a soft foam ball.

THE EXPERIENCE

Ask:

● **What kinds of things do you usually put in baskets?** (Laundry; easter eggs; plants.)

Say: **Our story today is about some men who put a friend in a basket.**

Tell the story of Paul's escape in a basket, found in Acts 9:23-25.

Ask:

● **How many friends do you think it would take to lower Paul from the wall in a basket?**

● **How do you think Paul felt as his friends lowered him over the wall?** (Scared they might drop him; glad he had friends to help him escape.)

Say: **Paul's friends had to work together to help him escape. We're going to play a game in which we'll have to work together in teams.**

Spread the bedsheet across the floor. Have the children line up along the sheet's two long sides and hold the edges of the sheet. Have the children on each side work as a team.

Say: **I'll toss the ball into the center of the sheet. Try to toss the ball off the sheet onto the floor on the other team's side. No hands may touch the ball. You may hold only the sheet. When the** ball falls onto the floor, I'll put it back in the center of the sheet, and we'll start again.

Let the children play the game several times, then have them sit down. Ask:

● **Was it easy or hard to get the ball onto the floor on the other team's side? Why?** (Easy, because we worked together; easy, because we shook the sheet really hard; hard, because we had to get the ball between people when they were sitting close together.)

● **How did you help your team?** (I held part of the sheet; I shook the sheet; I kept the ball from falling off.)

● **How is that like the way you help your friends?** (Sometimes we work together on projects; we play together on sports teams; we talk to each other.)

● **Why do we need friends?** (To listen to us; to play with us; to encourage us; to pray for us.)

● **How can you be a good friend?** (Help my friends if they need it; listen to my friends; cheer my friends up when they're sad.)

Say: **Paul's friends actually helped save his life. Good friends help us in many ways. Let's look for ways to help our friends this week.**

Bandannas

- -

PREPARATION

You'll need:

● **two 18×18-inch squares of plain cloth for each child,**

● **fabric markers or paints,**

● **and old newspapers.**

● **If you have pinking shears, use them to cut the cloth squares.**

● **Before class, contact a local children's home or other charitable organization and arrange to donate the bandannas your kids will be making. If you want to donate additional items, let the children and their parents know in advance.**

STORY

Dorcas is raised from death (Acts 9:36-43)

Dorcas helped needy people. Many people were sad when Dorcas died, so Peter prayed for her, and she came to life again. Children will learn that they can make a difference in needy people's lives, just like Dorcas did.

THE EXPERIENCE

Ask:

● **What are our clothes made from?** (Wool; cotton; fabric; buttons; zippers.)

● **Where do you get your clothes?** (At the store; from my older sister; my mom makes them.)

Say: **We're going to hear a story about a woman who made clothes to give away.**

Tell the story of Dorcas, found in Acts 9:36-43.

Ask:

● **What do you think Dorcas was like?** (Kind; friendly; like my grandma.)

● **Tell about a kind, friendly person that you know.**

Say: **Dorcas made clothing for needy people. We're going to** make bandannas to help us remember this story. We'll make one to keep and one to give away.

Spread newspapers across the work area and set out the fabric markers or paint. Give children each two squares of cloth and show them how to make designs on their bandannas by drawing and painting circles, triangles, squares, and other shapes on the cloth.

As children are working, ask:

● **Why do you think Dorcas was always doing good and helping needy people?** (She knew they needed help; she wanted to be like Jesus.)

● **How can we help needy people?** (Give food; give clothes; be friendly.)

Say: **Sometimes even people who have food and clothing need our help. How could you help a sick person?** (Visit them; send a get-well card.)

● **How could you help an elderly person?** (Visit them; read to them; help take care of their yard or house.)

Say: **We can help needy people, just like Dorcas did. Our class will help by giving our bandannas and the other things you've brought to needy children in our area. Look for ways you can help needy people this week.**

Prayer Partners

STORY

Peter escapes from prison (Acts 12:1-19)

Peter was thrown into prison for following Jesus. While Peter was in prison, his friends met together to pray for him. One night an angel appeared and led Peter out of the prison. When children see how God answered the prayers of Peter's friends, they'll be encouraged to pray for their friends.

THE EXPERIENCE

Say: **After Jesus died, his followers became known as Christians. The countries where they lived didn't like Christians and tried to arrest and even kill people who taught about Jesus and worshiped Jesus. Our story today is about someone who was put in prison for following Jesus.**

Have the children stand together in a cluster as you tell the story of Peter's escape from prison, found in Acts 12:1-19. When you tell about Peter being chained, wrap the toilet paper or crepe paper around the group of children. When you tell about Peter's chains falling off, encourage the children to break through the toilet paper or crepe paper. Have them sit down while you tell the rest of the story.

PREPARATION

You'll need:

● **photocopies of the people cutout pattern (p. 104),**

● **paper,**

● **pencils,**

● **crayons or markers,**

● **and a roll of toilet paper or crepe paper.**

● Before class, photocopy enough patterns so each child can have one.

Ask:

● **How did God answer Peter's friends' prayers?** (God sent an angel; God helped Peter escape from prison.)

● **How can we pray like Peter's friends prayed?** (Be serious about our prayers; pray a lot; pray together with our friends or family.)

● **How can we remind ourselves to pray for our friends?** (Put notes around to remind us; ask someone to help us remember.)

Say: **We're going to make prayer-partner cutouts to remind us to pray for friends in this class.**

Form pairs. Distribute paper, pencils, and people cutout patterns. Have children each fold their paper into four panels, accordion-style, trace around the people cutout pattern, and then cut it out. Make sure children position the pattern correctly on the fold. Have them each write their name and something they'd like to pray about on one person and write their partner's name and prayer request on the other person.

Say: **Peter's friends prayed together for him. We can pray together for our friends. Let's pray for our friends now.**

Close by having the children complete this sentence prayer with the name of their prayer partner: Dear God, Please be with my friend _____ this week.

Encourage children to take home their prayer-partner cutouts to remind them to pray for their partners this week.

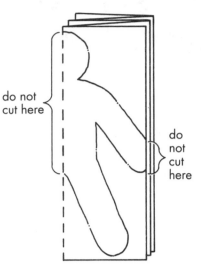

do not cut here

do not cut here

Dyed Wind-Flags

STORY

Lydia becomes a Christian (Acts 16:11-15)

Paul and his companions went outside the city of Philippi to teach about Jesus. When they saw a group of women gathered near the river, they sat down and talked with them. As a result of Paul's teaching, Lydia became a Christian. Use this story to teach children the importance of meeting together with other Christians.

THE EXPERIENCE

Ask:

● **What's your favorite thing about meeting together at church?** (Singing songs; reading the Bible; seeing my friends.)

Say: **We're going to make dyed wind-flags that will help us remember to meet together, then we'll hear a story about a woman who sold a special kind of dyed cloth.**

Cover the work area with newspapers. Set out bowls of rubbing alcohol and let the children drip 20 or more drops of red food coloring into one bowl and 20 or more drops of blue food coloring into the other bowl.

PREPARATION

You'll need:

● two bowls,
● rubbing alcohol,
● red and blue food coloring,
● round coffee filters,
● markers,
● newspaper,
● scissors,
● large yarn needles,
● and string.
● Before class, pour ¼ cup of rubbing alcohol into each bowl and thread the string through the yarn needles.

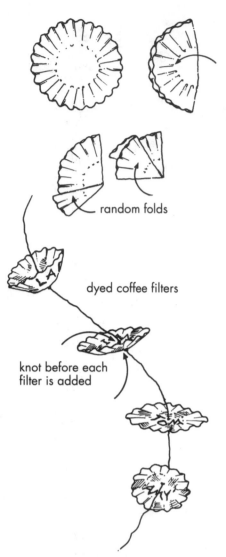

random folds

dyed coffee filters

knot before each
filter is added

Distribute markers and have children each write their name on four coffee filters. Demonstrate how to fold the filters at random and dip the folded sections into the bowls of colored rubbing alcohol. Lay the filters on the newspaper to dry.

As the filters are drying, tell the story of Lydia, found in Acts 16:11-15. After the story, ask:

● **Why do you think the women were meeting together?** (They were friends; they wanted to talk to each other.)

● **Why is it important for us to meet together here at church?** (So we can share what we learn about God; so we can find out how to help each other; so we can pray and worship together.)

Say: **God wants us to meet together today, just like Lydia and the women met together a long time ago. To help us remember our friends at church, trade coffee filters with three friends. When you're through trading, you should have four different people's filters, including your own.**

Wait for children to exchange filters, then demonstrate how to make a wind-flag. Give children each a threaded yarn needle and show them how to run the needle and string through the center of one filter all the way to the knot. Help children tie another knot about 5 inches from the knot they've just tied. Demonstrate how to run the string through the next filter all the way to that knot. Continue to help children add filters to the string, until they have all four filters in place. Have them tie a knot above the last filter. Encourage children to tie their wind-flags to a tree or fence post in their yard when they get home.

Say: **Paul wanted to meet with other people to worship and to talk about Jesus. We meet to worship, to encourage each other, and to talk about Jesus. Each time you see your wind-flag, you can remember your three friends and look forward to the times we meet together.**

Missionary Map

STORY

Paul's missionary journeys (Acts 13:1-12; 14:1-20; 16:6-10)

Paul had many adventures as he traveled to tell others about Jesus. In Cyprus, he met a sorcerer, in Lystra and Derbe people tried to kill him by stoning him, and in Troas he had a vision of a Macedonian man begging for help. Hearing about Paul's adventures will interest children in the work of missionaries today. If your church supports any missionaries, be prepared to tell the children about them.

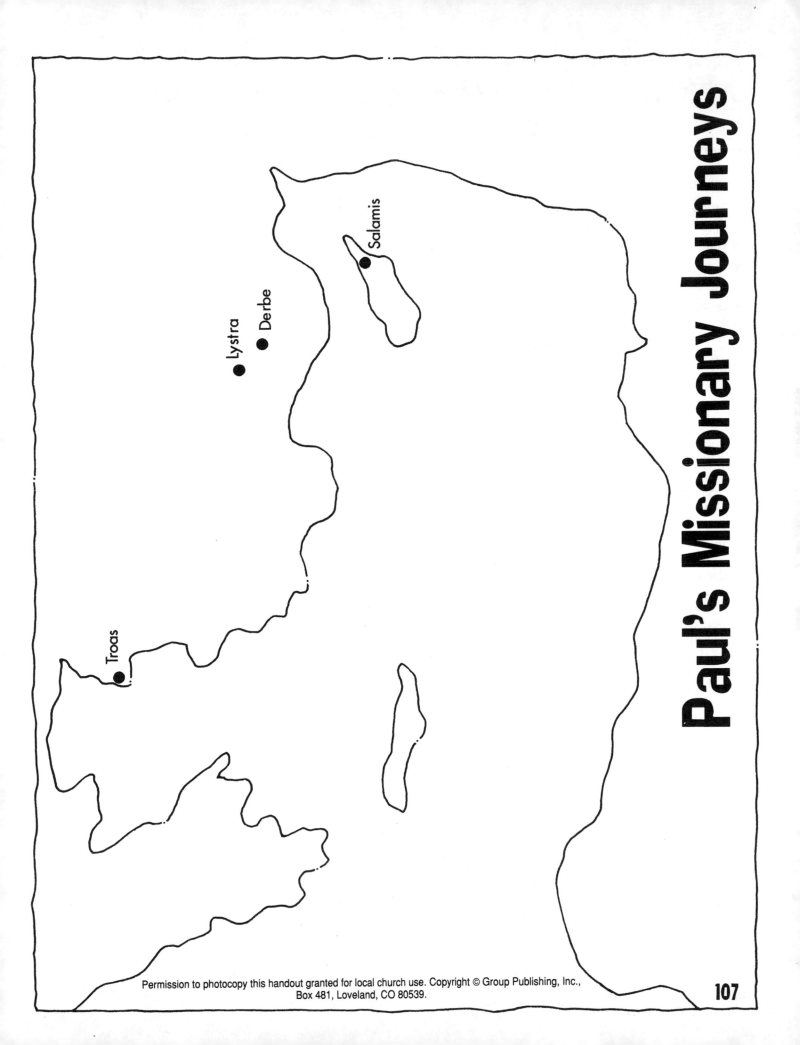

Paul's Missionary Journeys

Salamis

Lystra
Derbe

Troas

PREPARATION

You'll need:

- large bowls and mixing spoons,
- salt,
- flour,
- water,
- cooking oil,
- green food coloring,
- measuring cups,
- poster board,
- glue,
- pencils,
- paper towels,
- toothpicks,
- copies of the map outline on page 107,
- and a map of Paul's missionary journeys (found in the map section of many Bibles).
- Cut the poster board into four quarters. Make four copies of the map outline and glue a copy to each section of the poster board. You may want to enlarge the map slightly.

THE EXPERIENCE

Ask:

● **What does a missionary do?** (Tells people about Jesus; goes to other countries.)

Say: **Paul was a missionary in Bible times. We're going to make a map of some of the countries he traveled to.**

Form groups of no more than five. Show each group how to make salt dough by measuring and mixing 3 cups flour, 1 cup salt, ¾ cup water, ¼ cup cooking oil, and green food coloring. You may need to mix additional dough as the children are working.

Have each group fill in the land sections on their map with dough. Remind children to fill in the island of Cyprus.

Show children the map of Paul's missionary journeys and help them mark the locations of Salamis, Lystra, Derbe, and Troas with toothpicks. When groups have marked these cities on their maps, tell them about the events that occurred in each of these cities. The accounts of these events are found in Acts 13:1-12; 14:1-20; 16:6-10.

Ask:

● **Why do you think Paul became a missionary?** (He wanted other people to know Jesus; to obey Jesus.)

● **How do you think it would feel to be a missionary in another country?** (Fun; scary; exciting.)

● **Why do we want other people to know about Jesus?** (Because Jesus loves them; because Jesus told us to tell people about him.)

● **How can you help missionaries?** (Pray for them; send them letters; give money to help them pay for the things they need.)

Say: **Paul had many great adventures as he traveled to tell people about Jesus. Missionaries today have great adventures, too. But sometimes missionaries get lonely or afraid, just like you do. We can encourage and help missionaries by praying for them.**

Lead children in praying for the needs of your church's missionaries. If you are working outside of a church setting, thank God for all the people who tell others about Jesus in your city and around the world.

Go to Jail

PREPARATION

You'll need:

- a pencil and a half sheet of typing paper for each child,
- tape,
- and markers.

STORY

Paul and Silas in jail (Acts 16:16-40)

Paul and Silas sang and prayed to God, even while they were in jail. During an earthquake, they taught the jailer about Jesus. Children will learn from Paul and Silas' example to trust God even when they have problems.

THE EXPERIENCE

Ask:

● **What would it be like to be in an earthquake?**

Say: **Our story today is about a miraculous earthquake.**

Tell the story of Paul and Silas in jail, found in Acts 16:16-40.

Say: **Now we're going to put someone in jail in a very unusual way.**

Distribute typing paper and markers. Have children fold their typing paper in half and draw prison bars on one side and a face on the other side. Distribute pencils and have children tape their folded papers over the top of the pencil. They may also want to tape the outside edges together. Show children how to roll the pencil between their palms. The face should appear to be behind bars.

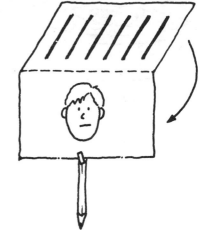

Ask:

● **Paul and Silas didn't deserve to be put in jail. What would you feel like if you were put in jail, but you hadn't done anything wrong?** (Angry; frustrated; worried.)

● **Why do you think Paul and Silas prayed and sang in jail?** (They trusted God to take care of them; they were trying to keep from worrying or getting angry.)

● **Paul and Silas prayed and sang in jail to show their trust in God. What can you do to show your trust in God when you have problems?** (Pray about the problem; read the Bible to see how to handle the problem; keep going to church.)

Say: **Paul and Silas worshiped God even while they were in jail. Even though things looked bad, they knew God was taking care of them. No matter how big our problems may be, we can trust God to take care of us, too.**

Riding a Storm

STORY

Paul's shipwreck (Acts 27)

Paul's ship was struck by a storm that lasted 14 days. But Paul remained calm and encouraged other people on board. Children will learn from this story that they can trust God when they encounter problems in life.

THE EXPERIENCE

Tell the story of Paul's shipwreck, found in Acts 27.

Say: **Paul took an exciting voyage in a storm. Now let's make storms of our own.**

Give children each an unshelled peanut. Help children each open the

PREPARATION

You'll need:

● paper or plastic bowls,
● water,
● a measuring cup,
● a teaspoon,
● unshelled peanuts,
● baking soda,
● vinegar,
● and plastic spoons.

peanut shell boat

shell so it comes apart in two long halves. Tell them they may eat the peanuts inside.

Distribute paper bowls and pour ½ cup of water into each bowl. Have children put their peanut shell halves on the water as boats. Help children each add one teaspoon of baking soda to their bowl and stir. Then help them add one teaspoon of vinegar and watch the "waves." When the bubbling stops, let children add another spoonful of vinegar.

As children are working, ask:

● **How do you think Paul felt during the storm?** (Afraid; excited; glad he could trust God to take care of him.)

● **How do you think the other men felt?** (Afraid; worried; excited.)

● **When you have problems, do you feel more like Paul or the other men? Why?** (I feel like Paul because I know I can trust God; I feel like the other men because I always get worried.)

● **How can we feel calm when we have problems?** (Trust God; pray; read the Bible; think about good things.)

Read Philippians 4:6-7. If you have older children in your class, ask a volunteer to read it.

Say: **Paul had peace during the storm because he trusted God. If we trust God, we can have that kind of peace, too—even when we face problems.**

Fruit of the Spirit Mural

PREPARATION

You'll need:

● butcher paper,

● markers,

● glue,

● and confetti.

● You can make confetti by tearing or cutting colored construction paper or by using a hole punch to punch circles in colored paper.

STORY

The fruit of the Spirit (Galatians 5:22-23)

Paul told the Galatians that the Holy Spirit produces love, joy, peace, patience, kindness, goodness, faithfulness, gentleness, and self-control. Discussing this passage will deepen children's understanding of the fruits of the spirit and encourage them to ask God to produce these fruits in their lives.

THE EXPERIENCE

Say: **As Paul traveled, he often wrote letters to the churches he had visited. These verses are from the letter he wrote to the Galatian church.**

Read Galatians 5:22-23. If you have older children in your class, ask a volunteer to read it.

Roll butcher paper across the floor. Form no more than nine groups and assign each group one or more of the qualities listed in the passage.

Say: **We're going to make a fruit-of-the-Spirit mural. I'm going to assign each group a quality that makes up the fruit of the Spirit. Write the name of your quality in large letters on the bottom of your section of the butcher paper. Then draw a piece of fruit, such as an orange or a banana, to represent your fruit of the Spirit quality. Talk to your friends in your group about your quality. When we're all done, I'll ask your group to tell the class about your drawing.**

Distribute markers and have children draw a large piece of fruit on their section of the butcher paper. Help children write the names of the qualities that make up the fruit of the Spirit in large letters on the butcher paper. Then distribute glue and confetti and help groups outline their letters with glue and cover the glue with confetti. Let the mural dry before you hang it up.

As children are working, circulate among the groups and monitor the discussions of the fruit of the Spirit. If groups seem stumped, use the following definitions to help them understand their qualities:

Love—liking someone; putting someone else first

Joy—happiness; gladness

Peace—calmness; not being upset or worried

Patience—waiting without complaining

Kindness—doing good to someone

Goodness—doing what is right and helpful

Faith—being loyal; always being a friend

Gentleness—being kind and caring

Self-control—taking charge of yourself

When children have finished working, have groups tell the class about the qualities they talked about and illustrated. When all groups have shared, say: **Find a partner and tell your partner one way you'll try to show the fruit of the Spirit to others this week.**

Give the children a few minutes to complete this activity, then call the group back together. Close by having children complete the following sentence prayer: "Dear God, Help me to show _____ this week. Amen."

NEW RESOURCES FROM *Group*...

Snip-And-Tell Bible Stories

Karyn Henley

Your children will watch in awe as Bible stories literally unfold before their very eyes. Each Bible story has a photocopiable pattern for you to fold and cut as you tell the story. The figures you create are key parts of the story, such as...

- the snake, the tree, and the fruit from the Garden of Eden (Genesis 3);
- Moses in the basket (Exodus 1—2:10);
- Samson and his hair—which you cut off (Judges 16);
- the lion from Daniel and the lions' den (Daniel 6);
- a string of wise men (Matthew 2:1-12);
- Jairus' daughter sitting up in bed (Mark 5:21-43);
- the fish from when Jesus fed 5,000 people (John 6:1-13);

...and more stories from both the New and Old Testaments!

Photocopiable patterns let you practice cutting and telling the story ahead of time—and patterns are easy to follow. The solid lines show you where to cut, while the dotted lines show you where to fold. And discussion questions about the story allow you to get the children involved—by having younger children help tell the story if they know it—or having older children help cut and fold the patterns.

1-55945-192-0 $12.99

Children's Ministry Clip Art

Mary Lynn Ulrich

Add pizazz and style to your ministry with creative clip art. Use these lively illustrations in newsletters, fliers, letters, and on bulletin boards—anywhere you need to grab kids'—and parents'—attention.

With this creative art, you can...
- design fabulous fliers and handouts for meetings on dozens of topics,
- announce upcoming events with zany, attention-getting calendars, and
- promote specific children's ministry programs.

This giant collection of clip art will add a professional touch to your children's ministry. It's as easy as 1-2-3.
                    1—Choose your art   2—Cut it out   3—Paste it down
and your publicity is ready to photocopy!

ISBN 1-55945-018-5 $15.99